Jesus' Words without Inflammation

By Dave Paul Campbell

Copyright 2021

This work is considered non-fiction; however, some of the passages contain fictional stories. Names, characters, places, and incidents are either the product of the author's imagination or are used fictitiously. Unless specifically named, resemblance to any persons, living or dead, business establishments, events, or locales is entirely coincidental.

Jesus' Words without Inflammation

Published: Kindle Direct Publishing Platform

Cover art: Dave Paul Campbell

First Printing: April 2021
Printed in the United States of America
First Edition: April 2021

CONTENTS

About the Author

Dave Campbell lives near Seattle and is a seasoned minister/counselor. He traveled for many years, singing and evangelizing in the Northwest. He made several appearances on TBN's local Praise the Lord program as well as other television appearances in Alaska, Seattle, and Vancouver areas. When Dave stopped touring, he became a children's pastor and began introducing innovative techniques for bringing the Bible to life for young minds. After a miraculous touch of God at a local camp meeting, he launched "Joy of Freedom" outreach ministry and pastored it for 9 years. The outreach is still ministering to the homeless, destitute, and chemically dependent individuals, today.

Among many pastoral privileges, Dave has spent many hours counseling people with severe life issues. The experience he has gained for practical life applications of Biblical principles has been invaluable. Dave brings many things to the counseling table, including good common sense and a ground-roots approach to difficult and sensitive challenges.

Contact Information: info@davecampbellbooks.com

Website: davecampbellbooks.com

Also, find *Dave Paul Campbell* on Facebook.

Foreword

In all of the end-times study, why isn't Jesus considered to be the number one authority for prophecy? To form desired doctrines, it seems the Son of God is put aside when it comes to pivotal points of future-telling. Dave thinks it is time we take a hard look at what Jesus actually said – and what he didn't say. Once we can lock into what Jesus was trying to tell his disciples, we can form a solid base for other texts to build on. After all, who knew the future better than Christ?

This is Dave's second book in a short series on simple eschatology. The first was Revelation without Inflammation, which introduced a set of study tools that Dave also uses in this book. These simple rules include the RID method and focus on a fresh, simple read of the text as literature, rather than a spiritual recipe. This provides a way to explore without chaos while preserving the reader's right to think independently. Dave takes this approach because he desires to let Jesus' words stand on their own without manipulation. As a result, readers may be amazed at what Jesus really said – and, again, what he did not say. With this system, many people can see important keys to prophetic meaning, and marvel at things they may not have seen before. Is this because there are deeply intertwined mysteries in what Jesus said? No, it is because many scholarly "explanations" have clouded what Jesus said. Dave believes that by using plain English, the sentences and paragraphs clearly state certain undeniable facts.

Dave invites you to come with him on this exploratory journey. Dare to see Jesus' words from a fresh, new perspective.

Chapter 1

Less Craziness, Please

Here is a culinary fact: Simply adding more ingredients to food does not guarantee a better flavor. Similarly, adding text or ideas to what is written in the Bible does not guarantee truth or accuracy. In fact, one tactic that chronic liars use is to create large fanciful tales, built on layers of mixed truth and fiction. Now, I am sure that most serious Bible scholars are not trying to introduce errors in Biblical doctrines, but many can become so enthusiastic about their beliefs that they lose sight of what is written on the pages. Thus, there comes a time, when we need to just clear all the smoke and go back to the basics.

In my former book, my dear Theophilus… Okay, wait, this is not the book of Acts, and I don't think I know anyone named Theophilus. What I need to say is that in one of my previously published books, REVELATION WITHOUT INFLAMMATION, I presented a method and a case for looking at a difficult text in a simple manner. In the first part of that book, I said,

If the Book of Revelation was a living organism, it would be so inflamed that it would likely die.

Why? Because, it has become so bloated, manipulated, and "Hollywood-ized" that it is nearly impossible to separate the truth from fantasy. The same is true of other prophetic passages in the Bible. Jesus' own words have been twisted to mean nearly anything that man can imagine. Somehow, somewhere, there must be a way to pierce through all this hype and truly see what the writer intended – or at least, what he did not intend.

As we study end times (eschatology), we need to consider what Jesus said about the future of those living in his time. After all, the Son of God should be the foremost expert when it comes to future events. And, we can go so far as to say that if there is any doubt about future events, what Jesus said should be the absolute defining factor. So, I have dedicated this book to the investigation of what Jesus said about end times, using the same techniques that we used in the study of Revelations. I think this will help you clean out the speculation, and twisted scriptures, and right down bad doctrine from your doctrinal "toolbox."

Now, does this mean I am going to throw more doctrine at you and declare it is the right thinking? Absolutely not. What we're going to do is figure out a simple way to clear out the junk, and dissipate the cloud that covers the beautiful words of Jesus. Once we do that, you will have a better chance of seeing what the author intended. From there, what conclusions you draw are strictly between you and Jesus – with no prophecy mongers to interfere.

When We Think We're Right

If you have lived very long on this planet, you have likely been in a situation where you were sure you were right, then discovered you were wrong. How about the opposite? Did you hear something that made you doubt your belief, then discover you were right after all? Well, I have good news for you. You're human! Living on planet earth can be confusing and sometimes even maddening, yet we all seem to take some level of pride in being right in our beliefs - and our beliefs don't even need to be religious. For instance, you can believe with all your heart and mind that you turned off the stove, yet it can still be on. One question that rolls around in my head is this: Why is it so important for people to be right, and why do we feel so badly when we're wrong? Could it be just a simple matter of pride? Let's explore this idea as we look at a lady who made a total commitment to her belief.

The Power of Green Stuff

A lady in our family (who shall remain unnamed) went to lunch with other family members at a local buffet. She was having a good time until she put a bite of some "green stuff" in her mouth and quickly started gasping. After much water and time, she was finally able to explain her intense discomfort. Apparently, when she saw a fairly large bowl of what looked like Guacamole, she took several heaping spoonfuls and deposited them on her food. Unfortunately, the green stuff was

Wasabi. Now, we can all laugh at her, and I'm pretty sure many family members did, but every one of us has been in a similar situation. We look at all the evidence and carefully deduce that certain things are facts. Once we're convinced of our facts, we act on them, wholeheartedly. Case in point, if the lady I mentioned had doubted even a little about the green substance she put on her plate, she would have tasted a tiny portion of it before committing to a large bite. Obviously, she wholeheartedly believed that the green stuff was something different than it was.

The Altar of Truth

There are many views, beliefs, and interpretations of God's Word - and then there is what the writer meant. Clearing all the man-made smoke is not always easy, but some tools make the job a little easier (we will talk about those a little later). One thing is clear to me: The most important truths in the Bible are repeated and presented in simple ways that anyone can understand. This proves to me that God is fair and just and that he wants to connect personally with each of us. Perhaps this is an indication that our first tool for clearing away all the preconceived ideas about the Bible is to simply read it like we would any other book and try to see what the actual text says, without manipulation. There's a principle that goes along with this method and it goes something like this: If we care about what God is trying to say to us, sooner or later we will need to sacrifice our pet doctrines on the "Altar of Truth." No matter what we believe, or have been taught, if we want to get to what matters, we need to put it all in the "fire" so it can be tested. What survives the test of truth's fire, is what you want to hold onto. What is destroyed, is what needs to be trashed anyway and what is charred needs to be re-examined with a better microscope. Does this sound like a good and sound practice? I think it is and I have proven that it works over a very long time.

Now, in all fairness, I must give credit to where it is due. I am not the author of this idea about the "Altar of Truth." At one time in my life, I was trying to answer difficult questions about some scriptures in the Bible. I found that some things I had been taught didn't seem to have a very firm base in scripture. As I dug deeper, I also discovered wonderful truths about some of the things I had long believed. Along this path of discovery, however, I also discovered what I call "black holes" in traditional doctrines. It was about this same time, I heard Hank Hanegraaff (Bible Answer Man) on the radio, talking about the idea of "placing pet doctrines on the Altar of Truth." Since this was already beginning to happen in my life, I was encouraged to continue the journey. What followed was an ongoing exploration of the Bible with a new set of glasses that helped me see some awesome truths in God's Word and also see the outlines of false doctrines that had no real substance. Now, to be transparent, I've not been able to find this "Altar of Truth" quote from any other source, so I can't be certain whether Hank Hanegraaff was quoting someone else or whether it was something our Lord showed him, but for this book, I want to thank him for broadcasting what I consider to be a well-said truth.

A New Dress?

Though I may be a little uncertain about where the phrase "Altar of Truth" originated, there is a quote I am sure of:

"Old error in new dress is ever error nonetheless."

C.S. Lewis said this and I certainly could not have said it better. The truth is that since the time of the Apostles, there have been many heresies in the Christian community, yet there are no new ones - just the same old ones in different clothes. With so many false teachings out there, finding the real truth can be daunting. I hope that this book will help you find simple ways to read prophetic scripture. If nothing else, I hope you can at least come to see what prophetic scripture is not. You may never see all the truth in a passage when you read it, but you can certainly weed out a lot of things that are not true and take a closer look at questionable things.

Perhaps it will help you to know some of the things I do when I read the Bible: As I read, and study God's Word, there are things I see that seem to connect to other scriptures. Exploring the clear connections between what I am reading and other scriptures that are similar can help bring clarity and definition to what I am reading. One thing I will admit: After years of study, there are some scriptures where you can almost "read between the lines" of what the writer said. However, no matter how many positive suspicions or private musings I may want to share with my close Christian friends, I never teach or preach what I can't prove in scripture. One very important thing I want to share with you is this: A long time ago, I stopped just repeating what I was taught and purposed to teach only doctrine that stands on absolutely firm, provable ground. I hope after reading this book that you, too, will take up this mantle, and teach only what you can firmly prove from Biblical text.

The Rules

Rules, rules, rules! None of us like a truckload of rules, right? But, without any guidelines, we could never even find our socks! This being said, let me make a promise to you: For this study, there will be very few rules. We will use only three simple rules and you can remember them by the acronym R.I.D (RID). I chose this acronym because what we want to do is RID ourselves of theory, manufactured doctrines, and manipulated scripture. Here is the definition of RID:

1. Read without prejudice

2. If it is weird, compare

3. Don't play God

Now, let's see what each one of these means:

Read Without Prejudice

Imagine for a moment you are a new Christian and you've never read the Bible. Each phrase and each verse is fresh and new. You haven't spent a lifetime in church, so you don't have a thousand sermons floating around in your head. As you read, you take in each idea, like you would read any other book. Yes, you have much more respect and awe for this book, because it is God's Word, but you don't automatically look for hidden meanings and you don't expect that what is said is anything more or less than what is written. In your enthusiasm, you hang on to every word, not wanting to miss anything.

Now, import this scenario into your Bible life. What is different? Let me suggest that you've probably heard the passage you are reading several times and heard many sermons about it. When you read it, all this stuff swims around in your head. It is hard to separate what the passage is actually saying from all the things you have been told. Your mind also wants to fill in the blanks and mold the passage into 21st-century America. So, the task here is to slow down – and I mean slow way down, and read each word like it was your first time. Instead of thinking about what you have heard, simply look at the verse and hear what it is saying. Perhaps the author is meaning exactly what he wrote. Imagine that, like in other books, a person is trying to communicate a simple idea through words! Okay, maybe that was a little sarcastic and likely a bit snarky, but we do a terrible disservice to the original manuscript and our soul when we immediately assume there is much more to a verse than what is on the page. So, when you are reading God's Word, always try to read just what is on the page, first, and try to read it like you have never seen it or heard about it before. This is what I call a "Fresh Read." If you want more information and demonstrations of this Fresh Read, see my book FRESH READ.

If it is Weird, Compare

Sometimes when you read a passage in the Bible, it sounds funny and is not quite clear. In these cases, just a little study, or further reading, usually clears up the confusion. But, prophecy is different. There are often visions or dreams. In them, some images represent people, nations, and events. In some cases, God says what they mean and in other cases, he does not. However, there are instances where God has said something to a nation and it has been taught to the people of that nation over many years (even many generations). When phrases and symbolism are embedded in culture this way, God does not have to explain what he means when he uses the same symbolic phrases again. So when we read the Bible and things sound a little weird, we need to remember that the Bible was written to other people, in another culture, at another time. So what was very clear to them, might not be as clear to us. Now, how do we resolve this issue? One way is to compare what we read with other verses in the Bible that have a similar phrasing or symbolism. If God says I am going to sound a trumpet and does not explain it, then we can look at other verses that refer to God blowing a trumpet (or God having a trumpet blown). Yes, it may take a little digging but it is not hard and it is not rocket science. Since the whole Bible is in digital format, searching for a specific phrase (even through all sixty-six books) is quick and painless. So, if a word or phrase you are reading seems weird, look for other uses. If the phrase was used in an Old Testament verse that was about judgment, then you can rightfully conclude that the author in the New Testament (who knew the Old Testament passages) is likely referring to judgment. You will be amazed how many times this approach works and you don't have to be an expert to spot the similarities. In this way, we also carry on the methods of Bible experts like R.C. Sproul, who taught that the Bible should be the best source for defining the Bible.

Don't Play God

For me, this is the biggest issue: People are constantly trying to figure out what they "feel" is an unfulfilled prophecy. Now there is little doubt that for Jesus' disciples, there are many future events that were foretold. They were warned about many things. Some of Jesus' foretelling seemed to be pretty clear to them, while others remained a mystery until they started coming to pass. But, whether Biblical text is read from their view or ours when symbols are uncertain, it is bad theology to simply assign what we think. So here is the simple rule for what I consider proper prophetic study:

If God didn't say, then neither should you!

What does this phrase mean? Simply this: There are many places in prophecy where God said, this symbol means something. In some cases, a powerful animal in a vision represented a nation. In other cases, a dream of certain food meant there was going to be a famine. These were things that God told those who were involved. The prophetic words of Jesus' are not much different. In some places, Jesus explains his symbolism – at other times he does not.

Here is something important: Notice that I did not say, in prophecy, the image was the other thing. In prophecies, the real object, person, or landscape is not actually shown. God seems to never show the view-screen of a future world. In Revelation, for instance, Jesus shows John figures that represent people, nations, and events. So, we need to be very careful that we don't play God and try to explain things that God did not. Here is another aspect: If the people John was writing to understood something he wrote because of phrases they were familiar with, that is different, but in cases where there is new symbolism, we need to leave it to what God wants us to know and what he doesn't. Here is a fact we must accept:

God has never told anyone, everything about their future.

At best, God gives us a glimpse of the future and only tells us what we need to know. When we use our own ideas to fill in prophetic gaps, it is a mistake. Here is one reason why: For hundreds of years, the religious experts in Israel/Judah looked at prophecies about the Messiah (Jesus). They thought they had the whole scenario figured out. They just knew how the Messiah would come, and what he would do. In turn, they taught the people what they had deduced. How did this all turn out? Not so good. When Jesus came, he fulfilled the prophecies differently than they had envisioned and as a result, the religious leaders rejected the Messiah. Thus, many people missed the first coming of the Messiah. So it stands to reason that if scholars of any age use the same kind of conjecture with Jesus' prophetic statements, they could miss what he truly said to his disciples.

Carts and Horses

One common, but somewhat antiquated phrase is "Don't put the cart before the horse." However, in America we don't see all that many horse-drawn carts, so the imagery may be a little hazy to most people. Because it is the right concept for what I am going to propose, I would like you to stop for a minute and picture a horse in your head. Once you have that image fully detailed, then imagine a horse carriage. Now, place yourself in the scene with these two objects. You are standing there on the side of the road and in front of you is this carriage and standing behind the carriage (facing the carriage) is the horse. A person is sitting in the carriage and they want to go into town, so to accommodate them you yell to the horse, giddy up! Now, in your mind, what happens with the horse and carriage after you yell this command? Hmm. In my mind, there are two probable results:

1. The horse completely ignores you and nothing happens.

2. The horse bolts; runs around the carriage; and takes off down the street, leaving the carriage behind.

Now, let's alter the scenario. The horse is still behind the carriage, but you have somehow hitched the horse's neck to the back of the carriage. Now, when you yell giddy up, what does the horse do? Hmm. Well, we could hope the horse would somehow, push the carriage, but have you ever seen a horse do this? Would the horse even try? Hmm - I am thinking at best the horse may just look at you with an expression of "You have got to be kidding!" So, I think we can rightfully say, that putting the cart in front and the horse in the back, is ridiculous and just does not work in any sensible scenario.

Now, you may be starting to wonder if there is a point here besides the lesson on how to hitch up a horse. The answer is YES. One of the simple, yet most important things to remember when considering prophecies is that they come in a God-purposed order. In other words, God spoke to men about the future, when he chose to do so. When he wanted to reveal more about that same future, then he often added more details later. In some cases, the closer the time came for certain events to occur, the more details were given. This becomes critical when studying scripture because when we are trying to define the meaning of images and odd terms, it is crucial to place the weight of the meanings on the later revelations. For example, if there is some confusion about things that seem to be similar in the Book of Revelation and the Book of Daniel, then we use Revelation to define what is shown in Daniel, not the other way around. This being said, it is acceptable for the overall meaning of symbols and terms to be homogenous. The meanings may sort of flow back and forth between two or more books. However, if there is any question between books about the details of the events, we should take God's later revelation as the more detailed. Thus, the more detailed account of future events trumps the lesser detailed account. As an overarching example: What Isaiah, Ezekiel, or Daniel wrote about the future was more defined by what Jesus said to his disciples, and what Jesus said to his disciples was then even more defined by what he told/showed John on the Island of Patmos.

The Darby Ingredient

Whenever we decide to study Revelation, we're always faced with the influence of strong church figures who have published their ideas years before. Perhaps one of the most influential figures is John Nelson Darby. He was born in Westminster, London in 1801 and helped form the Plymouth Brethren church/organization. His background is interesting, but it seems that during a time when he was breaking away from the Anglican church and after a nasty fall off of a horse (in 1827), he began writing what could be described as theories about the meaning of certain scripture passages. What emerged, in part, was a million-dollar word that few of the young Sunday morning church attendees have heard: Dispensationalism.

Dispensationalism

Yes, it is a big word and it is had a huge effect in our modern church world. What does it mean? Here is my shortened definition: The theory or doctrine seems to say that God dispenses his grace in measures. Pointing to important events in Biblical history, this doctrine claims that they prove God pours out his grace in special favor at the times of his choosing and then pulls it back until another time of his choosing. Now, to be honest, I've always thought this a bit strange, because it seems to me that the Bible tells us that God's love never fades or diminishes. If his grace is driven by his love (and it is), then how can his grace diminish; thus how can it be poured out at one time in history and then pulled back at other times? Now, you can believe what you wish and you very well may be right, but I would like to offer another possible explanation: Perhaps God's chosen actions have nothing to do with the strength of his grace. Perhaps his historical timing is just that; crucial and strategic timing that capitalizes on cultures and events to maximize impact. Perhaps God is working very actively, every day, as he always has, for all men and making his grace known to all who seek him.

Along with the establishment of Dispensationalism, there was also Pre-Millennialism and an upsurge in Futurism. Wow, more fancy words. To make it short, this simply means Darby taught that Christians were going to be taken away, or "raptured," before a 7 year tribulation period. His base of futurism beliefs claimed that the book of Revelation was all or mostly about events that were to happen at a future date (after the early 1800s). What is odd about what he taught, is that no other Christian church taught or believed those things. In fact, it seems that no Christian church in history ever believed the doctrine he started teaching. So, guess what happened? He was branded as a heretic and his teaching was rejected by the Christian church. However, he didn't stop teaching it and trying to gain followers. The era when this new doctrine was launched was in the 1830s and it stayed fairly small in impact until 1909. So, it seems that for about sixty years, Darby's doctrines were not widely accepted and they might have even been in danger of falling into obscurity. However, in 1909 a remarkable thing happened. A respected Theologian by the name of Cyrus Ingerson Scofield published his study bible that included much of Darby's doctrines. Of course, what happens when people have a Bible where on the same page as scripture, there is an explanation of the passage? It makes those notes much more believable and in some ways, for some people, it makes the explanations nearly as authoritative as the Bible text.

Now, where did I get all this information? Did I make this up or get it from some questionable conspiracy website? No. I just did a simple search on the internet and cross-checked information from what seemed to be reliable sources (and there were several). So check it out and see for yourself. I think you will find the same or similar information about Mr. Darby and Mr. Scofield.

The Impact

It wasn't long after Darby's doctrines were popularized by Scofield's Study Bible, that Christian churches started teaching this new and exciting doctrine. Slowly, but surely, the doctrine that was once hailed as heresy, became the main-stream theories of tribulation, rapture, and the millennial reign of Christ. In more recent times, a flood of books, movies, and training materials have been produced that support Darby's unique doctrine.

So, what are we to do with this Dispensationalism when we look at Revelation? Well, the bottom line is that we shelf it during the study, until after we have looked at everything objectively. Does this mean you can't or shouldn't believe Darby's claims? No, this is not what I am saying. Even if some prophecies have already occurred somewhere in history, these prophecies could occur again. There are other instances in God's Word, where a prophecy was fulfilled and yet it was also to be fulfilled at another time. The real issue we have in making sure things are placed on the Altar of Truth is that whatever we believe needs to be well proven in scripture. If we have to manipulate and twist things to make them fit what we believe to be true, then we have violated a most sacred responsibility to seek the truth.

Remember this: I'm not writing this book to tell you what to believe or to preach a doctrine. I am trying to give you the tools to explore God's word purely, without preconceived influence. When you look at God's Word in this manner, you won't suddenly wake up and say, hey the Bible is all different than I was taught. You will more likely say, oh, I now see that some passages are clearer than they were before.

An Example from Revelation

Here is one last thing I would like to say about Jesus' prophetic words. When we look at the end of Revelation (21:18-19 - NIV), there is a warning:

"I warn everyone who hears the words of the prophecy of this scroll: If anyone adds anything to them, God will add to that person the plagues described in this scroll. And if anyone takes words away from this scroll of prophecy, God will take away from that person any share in the tree of life and in the Holy City, which are described in this scroll."

Pretty ominous warning, right Yet, it seems like every year someone comes up with a new slant on Revelation or there's a new movie that tries to show how events would happen in Revelation. I am pretty sure if we examine those movie scripts, we will find that most of the text is not from the Bible; much less from Revelation. Now, I can't speak for God, but it sure seems to me that our church world has majorly violated this warning. I thank God that we have forgiveness under Christ, but we need to realize that this warning was not placed there idly. God means what he says. He is serious about consequences when we change his Word and then present it as what he said. As this is true with the Book of Revelation, so it may be true with what the Son of God told his disciples. There may not be a "label" in the Gospel Books warning us to not change the text, but we still need to dedicate ourselves to preserving the accuracy of the manuscript, as it was written. The best way we can do this is to stop reading things into the text, and instead, see what we can extract from it.

A Side Note about Translations

Before we get into this study, I'd like to touch on the subject of Bible translations. For this book, I primarily use text from the New International Version (NIV). Many people cling vigorously to the King James Version and others prefer other modern translations. I stick to the NIV when I am teaching for two main reasons: First, it was specifically created to be readable. It was not designed to be the most accurate word-for-word translation; it was made to be as accurate as possible while still being easily readable to the average American. Second, the NIV was translated using all the available manuscripts in the world. In addition to using more resources than had ever been used before, a team of Biblical scholars and Theological experts were gathered to help edit and review the translation. Since the review team was made up of people from several different denominations, the translation avoided severe doctrinal swings that may have tainted the translation toward a specific group's beliefs.

Whatever translation you use is fine, as long as it was made by people who were concerned about accuracy. One caution about the older King James Version: Though it is quite accurate to the manuscripts it was taken from, the English words and phrasing are about 400+ years old and many of them have changed their meaning. To put it bluntly: We just don't talk that way anymore or use those phrases in the same way. My second caution is about paraphrases. There are some versions of the Bible (not many) that are paraphrased. That is, they took another translation and put it in their own words. So it is a kind of personal translation of what someone thought another translation meant; thus, it was not translated from the original text. This can produce some interesting slants and errors for those looking for the best study version. They can be helpful for young people who don't yet have a full mastery of the English language but for serious study, they are not recommended.

Chapter 2

First Things First

Analyzing the world around us is a common daily task that includes things both great and small. For instance, we can decide one moment that the milk in the refrigerator is not sour, then 15 minutes later decide whether it is safe to cross a busy street. The important thing to recognize in these given scenarios is that making a wrong conclusion about milk is usually not life-altering, whereas making a wrong conclusion about crossing the street can be deadly. What is important to see here is that we all make decisions based on our calculations.

Let's look at another example: Imagine you are driving on a two-lane road and you want to pass the slower car ahead of you. You look ahead - look at the terrain - guess how fast your car can go in a certain length of time - and thus calculate what your chances are of successfully pulling out into the oncoming lane. Now, let's say for argument's sake, you are 72% sure that you can successfully pass the car ahead of you. Notice that you don't take only 72% of yourself and leave 28% behind for safekeeping. No, you commit 100% of your being to a potentially dangerous situation, based on a 72% probability. This might seem like odd behavior when we stop and think about it, but the truth is that we make these kinds of decisions all the time.

While highways can be very dangerous, there are things in life that are even more critical to our survival. Think about war, terrorism, and even nuclear weapons. Pretty scary stuff, right? When we focus our attention on all that gloom and doom, we can become agitated, anxious, and eventually depressed. However, as deeply disturbing as these things are, there is still one aspect of survival that trumps them all: Life after this life. It seems to me that most people take very little time for making even a 72% calculation about where they are going after their death. More people I've talked to than not leave their eternal fate to a very big "maybe." It seems to me like the average American believes in some kind of cosmic roulette wheel, and they are pretty sure the number they have chosen will give them the winning spin. There's no evidence or indication they will be "okay" in the afterlife, yet they go happily on their way, oblivious of probable failure. To a Christian, this concept of throwing our eternal life to random chance should be tragic, and yet so many of us Christians similarly take a lackadaisical attitude toward our salvation. It is like we "bought" salvation like we would a car, then parked it in the driveway for all to see what a nice shiny toy we have. What follows, however, becomes spiritually unhealthy. Why? Because with this shiny new "toy" called salvation, we now go and live however we want, and say grace has covered it all so it doesn't matter. The problem I have with this is that I find no scriptural basis for this belief or attitude.

Does this sound a little preachy or condemning? It might be, but the real reason I said all this was to bring you to serious thinking about what is real and what is just popular. As a minister, I can say anything and someone somewhere will believe me. If I teach things that make people feel good, then they flock to my church; but where does the Bible come in? When do we put truth above what we want? These are interesting questions, but the truth is, it is a simple matter of choice.

The Story of Jesus at a Glance

Since most of what we know about Jesus was written in the first four books of the New Testament, it may be important to know some background on these books. One of the questions people always raise is the date of their writing. I think this is an obvious starting place since the credibility of the stories and their writers are key to accepting them as valid Christian texts. After all, if these four books were written 1800 years after Jesus lived on this planet, then we might conclude that the information could be highly inaccurate or even fabricated. In contrast, if these books were written within a generation of the events that occurred, and if the writers were eyewitnesses of the events or they talked to many reliable eyewitnesses, then the content of the books can more easily be trusted.

Here is what I could find on the internet about these writings:

**Some Bible scholars place the writings of
Mark as late as 70 AD; Matthew and Luke
around 80 to 90 AD, and John around 95 AD.
However, other scholars place Matthew's
writing as early as 40-45 AD.**

There is also some expert speculation that Matthew's book was at least partially built on Mark's writings (or possibly vice versa). Because the writings were so long ago, there will never be absolute proof as to the year of their writing. However, all (or nearly all) Bible scholars agree that the four gospel books were written in the first century AD. Thus, they were likely written by people who had seen the events themselves or they received them from other people who were eye-witnesses.

Now, as I said, debates about when the gospel books were written will never end, but if you're interested in exploring this further, you will need to sit down with your best cup of java juice and search the internet and/or read some books on the subject. Trust me about this, though: When you've come to the end of your studies, you probably will have little more than your personal belief to say the exact year these books were written. The harsh reality is that it is just been too long and there are not enough solid facts (outside the books) to say the exact year of its writing.

At this point, I would like to remind you that this book is not for providing all the answers about everything. I couldn't hope to fit all that in a single book, or even several volumes. This book intends to give you a method of study and an encouragement to take what is here and continue exploring on your own.

First Some Parables

To avoid confusion and conserve paper space, I will avoid copying the whole of all four gospel books into this book. Instead, I will highlight some of the scriptures that seem most important and leave the rest to you. Once you see how easy it is to apply the RID techniques, I am sure you will be studying other prophetic passages as well. I do promise to cover all the most controversial passages in this book, especially those that appear to address "end-times."

The first area we can look at is what Jesus said in some of his parables. Some readers may ask, why? So, I will address this question before we start: As we know, Jesus used story lessons to teach important principles about the Kingdom of God. Within these stories, he included information about who would enter this kingdom and who would not. He also seemed to talk about the demise of the Old Covenant and the establishment of the New Covenant. So, I believe it is important for us to look at the metaphoric way Jesus presented these things. The imagery and ideas may help us see the larger picture of what Jesus later told his disciples about the future (after he ascended). Now, as we look at these parables, we will compare the same parables as they appear in each of the Gospels. For budding Bible scholars, it may be interesting to note that there are no parables mentioned in the Book of John. Odd as it may seem, John seemed to focus more on other aspects of Jesus' life and ministry. Okay, it is time to dig in and look at our first parable and it is found in Matthew 13:24-30.

"Jesus told them another parable: "The kingdom of heaven is like a man who sowed

**good seed in his field. But while everyone
was sleeping, his enemy came and sowed
weeds among the wheat, and went away.
When the wheat sprouted and formed heads,
then the weeds also appeared. The owner's
servants came to him and said, 'Sir, didn't
you sow good seed in your field? Where then
did the weeds come from?' 'An enemy did
this,' he replied. The servants asked him,
'Do you want us to go and pull them up?'
'No,' he answered, 'because while you are
pulling the weeds, you may uproot the wheat
with them. Let both grow together until the
harvest. At that time I will tell the
harvesters: First, collect the weeds and tie
them in bundles to be burned; then gather
the wheat and bring it into my barn.'"**

Okay, now before we start speculating about the meaning of this passage, let's apply our RID study rules. First, let's pretend we have never seen this before. Without interjecting anything we have ever been told, what does this text say? Here's what I get (you may get something else): I see that Jesus is telling a story here, and I want to know what it is, piece by piece.

1. I am not sure where this story originates. I do know that teachers from all eras of time have used existing or traditional stories to explain certain principles. Common ideas and symbols were reused so the listeners could easily relate to what a teacher was instructing. This story may be original, or Jesus may

have brought in a story that the people knew, then altered it to meet his teaching purpose. Does it matter whether this story or a similar one was used before? Not in my thinking.

2. Jesus sets up this story by telling us that it is a comparison of the kingdom of God. So it seems that what Jesus says after this will all be about this idea.

3. This seems like a pretty simple story about a farmer who planted some seeds in a field that he owned. It seems he also had some enemies that purposely planted some weed seeds in his field. However, he didn't discover this until after the good seed (wheat) sprouted.

4. It becomes clear at this point that the owner of this field has servants. It seems the servants were the ones that discovered the problem and told the owner. They ask him what he wants them to do, and possibly suggest that they could go into the field and pull them all up. However, the owner says no, this would cause more damage than resolution.

5. The owner's solution was to wait until harvest. At that time the servants would be directed to harvest the weeds first and bind them, so they can be burned; then they were to gather the good plants (wheat) into the barn.

Now, if I summarized all this, I might say it this way: Jesus tells about a fictional farmer who plants wheat and then finds that people who hate him try to deny him his crop. In the end, the farmer employs a method to save his crop and destroy the unwanted weeds.

I'm not saying I have this all correct, but do you see what I did here? One thing I didn't do is bring in ideas of I suppose this or maybe that. I just read it like I would any other book and in my head, I summarized what I thought the author was trying to say. This is the first step in the RID concept and avoids importing outside ideas before the actual text is considered.

Now let's apply the second rule of RID. Is there anything weird or unfamiliar in this passage? Well, yes. Jesus sets up this story by telling us that it is a comparison to the kingdom of heaven. However, if we are coming into this passage for the first time, we may not know what Jesus is referring to. So, our first question might be, "What is the kingdom of heaven?" If we don't know what this kingdom of heaven is, then it is odd or unfamiliar, thus we need to look it up. The simplest approach is to search through a digital version of the Bible Text (free from the internet), using the phrase, "kingdom of heaven."

Here is what I discovered

1. There are over 30 verses in the Bible that have the phrase "kingdom of heaven." However, this exact phrase rarely appears in other books of the Bible. So, this terminology seems to be more unique to the writer of the Book of Matthew. The term kingdom of God, or "of the Lord" is used in a few other places in the Bible, but in many places where God's kingdom is mentioned, it is just referred to as the Kingdom. Perhaps one mystery here is that Mark uses the "kingdom of

heaven" in many places, but in at least one other place, he uses the phrase "kingdom of God." So, as a scholar, you will need to explore the scriptures to see if these two phrases refer to the same thing – or not. By doing a simple digital search of Bible text, using these two phrases, you can see how many times each was used and by what writers. By sampling some of the verses, you may see a pattern of use that suggests a difference between the phrases, or you may see that there is no practical difference in meaning. One other thing we can do here is looking words up in a Greek dictionary or word expository. I did just that and I found that in Greek, it seems this phrase is pretty generic: It seems a kingdom that is from or in the "heavens" is a celestial idea. To pagans, there were several gods in the heavens. Each one of them could have had a kingdom, or together, some may have shared the heavens as one ruling place or kingdom. So, perhaps, in contrast, the "kingdom of heaven," is more generic, whereas the "kingdom of God" (at least to the Jews) is more specifically the heavenly kingdom that belongs to, or is ruled by, Jehovah God.

2. Possibly the biggest clue to what this phrase means comes from Matthew chapters 3, 4, 5, and 9. Here is where we learn that John the Baptist came preaching "Repent for the kingdom of heaven is near." After John was imprisoned, Jesus began to preach the same message, and when Jesus sent out his disciples, he told them to preach "The kingdom of heaven is near." So part of the gospel message seemed to include this idea - and the logical conclusion that this kingdom is near the

people who needed to straighten out their lives and live in a Godly manner.

Once we consider what we found in text searches, we need to see if it helps us understand this phrase any better. If it does not, then sometimes, we need to step back and take a look at the bigger picture. When studying the first part of Revelation, it was not immediately clear about the significance of the seven churches in Asia. The text itself doesn't define much. However, when we look at where John says these churches are located and then look at a map, we discover that these churches were likely the closest ones to the Island of Patmos. They were on the mainland and positioned in two rows (from a satellite view). Looking at it from a lightly humorous way, from God's view the geographic layout was almost like John was a speaker in an amphitheater. If John could have had a loud enough sound system, he could have stood on the Island of Patmos and preached to his audience in Asia. In other words, the churches appeared to be placed like spectators in a theater, with two rows of seats, facing the Island. Of course, we can say this was just a coincidence, but was it? In a real sense, when John wrote the letters to the churches, they became, his (if they had not been before), thus, also his audience. The big point here is that sometimes taking in the big picture helps us get some clues to what the Bible text may be saying. Do we preach what we find on a map, or in another historical book? No. For doctrine, the Bible must be able to stand on its own. We can muse and theorize, but we do not teach what we cannot solidly prove within the pages of the Bible.

Regarding this bigger-picture scenario, let's go back to the book of Matthew. There is a bigger picture here that is contained within the Bible pages. I have mentioned it already, but the concept can slip away from us when we are not focused on it. Remember what John the Baptist was preaching? It was this principle that the kingdom of Heaven is near (Matthew 3:2). After John was not able to preach anymore, Jesus began to preach the same message (Matthew 4:12-17). However, depending on the translation, this phrase may mean something different than what we first suspect. When people read "The kingdom of heaven is near," they tend to hear "The kingdom of Heaven is coming soon." But, the Greek words don't say this. One clue is that the NIV version (and others) use the phrase, "Repent, for the kingdom of heaven has come near." John and Jesus, both used this phrasing. It was an action that included the recent past, now, and the future. It was something that was not a prophecy of future events. Thus, we might say in today's English, "God's kingdom is here, now. It has arrived." We also get a clue from Matthew 17:20-21.

> **Once, on being asked by the Pharisees when the kingdom of God would come, Jesus replied, "The coming of the kingdom of God is not something that can be observed, nor will people say, 'Here it is,' or 'There it is,' because the kingdom of God is in your midst."**

Here, it seems Jesus is even more clearly saying that the kingdom of God was there, right then, and that it was among them. So, let me ask you a question: Who was representing the kingdom of God or the kingdom of heaven on earth? The answer is obviously, Jesus. He is the one who is described as the "king of kings." When a king came into another country

(in ancient times), and had his envoy with him, it could be said
(at that time) that the country the king represented had "come."
So, in a real sense, John proclaimed (as the forerunner) that the
King had already arrived - so they needed to make preparations
for him (in their heart). Jesus continued to proclaim that he,
the King, had arrived – but no one fully understood what either
John or Jesus were saying. It was hidden from them.

Jesus Lifts the Veil

Now, before we go any further, we need to look at Jesus'
explanation of this parable. This is very important as the next
step in letting the Bible define itself. If we start assigning
meaning to this parable that grows out of our opinion, it may
not line up with what Jesus said it means. So, if you are
reading or have read this passage in Matthew, you may have
noticed that the disciples asked Jesus about its meaning. Of
course, if we jump into this parable from a reference book or
concordance, we may not see this explanation, because the
disciples wait until Jesus finished teaching a whole set of
parables before they asked for the meaning. Perhaps this was
out of courtesy, or perhaps where they were sitting was not
close enough to effectively interrupt his teaching. Either way,
Jesus did tell his disciples that he would only reveal the
meaning of parables to them.

Let's look at how Jesus explained this parable in Matthew
13:36-43:

> **Then he left the crowd and went into the
> house. His disciples came to him and said,
> "Explain to us the parable of the weeds in the**

field." He answered, "The one who sowed the good seed is the Son of Man. The field is the world, and the good seed stands for the people of the kingdom. The weeds are the people of the evil one, and the enemy who sows them is the devil. The harvest is the end of the age, and the harvesters are angels. "As the weeds are pulled up and burned in the fire, so it will be at the end of the age. The Son of Man will send out his angels, and they will weed out of his kingdom everything that causes sin and all who do evil. They will throw them into the blazing furnace, where there will be weeping and gnashing of teeth. Then the righteous will shine like the sun in the kingdom of their Father. Whoever has ears, let them hear.

Okay, since we are partnering in this study of Jesus' prophetic words, what did you get from Jesus' explanation? In all honesty, if you have heard many sermons and/or been in Bible studies very long, you will have heard a lot of teaching on this parable. I think the basic explanation is pretty clear. Jesus is planting the good seed, which is the Good News of God's salvation. Others in the world who are working for the "Evil One," are planting bad /evil messages that thwart the spreading of the Good News. Notice that Jesus says, "The field is the world, and the good seed stands for the people of the kingdom." Since Jesus is talking about people who are living at that time (or it includes them), the "people of the kingdom" seem to me to be the believers who have grown up as a result of the seed Jesus planted. They become "seeds" themselves.

So, here is yet another possible clue about the kingdom of heaven or the kingdom of God, that John and Jesus were preaching about. Of course, this calls for some deduction, so I will leave you to interpret it as you see it.

Now, since we are taking a fresh look at Jesus' prophetic teachings, we must consider the future aspect of what Jesus taught. We are only looking at this parable because it contains statements about the future of the people Jesus was talking to. So, let's take a close look at this portion of the parable:

> **"The harvest is the end of the age, and the harvesters are angels. "As the weeds are pulled up and burned in the fire, so it will be at the end of the age. The Son of Man will send out his angels, and they will weed out of his kingdom everything that causes sin and all who do evil. They will throw them into the blazing furnace, where there will be weeping and gnashing of teeth. Then the righteous will shine like the sun in the kingdom of their Father."**

What I see here is a foretelling of an event (or possibly more than one), where God's angels "harvest" the weeds (bad seed) and then the wheat (good seed). Those who insisted on spreading malicious messages that lead others astray were "burned up." This could be physical or spiritual (soul), but since in Christianity it is commonly believed that a soul lives forever and does not die, this seems it would be more likely physical destruction since it is "burned up" instead of in "pain and agony." Again, after your research, you can make your conclusions. Just be careful here to not read things into the text. Take it for what it says and nothing more.

Now, moving on to the remainder of this parable's explanation, it seems to me Jesus is saying that after the bad seed is destroyed, then the good seed can shine, and not be overshadowed or thwarted by the bad seed. One thing I did notice about this parable is there seems to be no specific talk about anyone going to heaven or hell. The good seed does not seem to be taken anywhere. Using just the text alone, it seems to me that it is saying the good seed will shine, where they are. The wheat is gathered, but left where it is, whereas the bad seed is gathered and burned up. Now, highly controversial questions here can be phrased something like this: Were the people who spread the bad seed punished with fire on this earth? Was this during Jesus' time or after? Were those who represent the good seed gathered together and protected to live on? If any historical events might satisfy this parable, is it possible Jesus was referring to those future events, verses a soul judgment after this life? Could it be both? Hmm. You need to study, study, study, my friend. The answers are likely there within the pages of your Bible.

BREAK

Okay, taking a close look at these parables can be quite tedious, so why don't you put the book down for a minute and get yourself a refreshing beverage – maybe even a "biscuit," as they say in the UK. Meanwhile, I will insert a little story, to break up the monotony.

I road my bike a lot when I was a teenager. I road it about half a mile or more to school and on my paper-route every day. Yep, I was a paper-boy. My route was not one of the longer ones, but even so, I had some interesting people and odd things on the route. One lady's last name was "Mrs. Speed." I don't think I had ever heard of anyone with that name before that, nor since. One of my customers had a pet crocodile. It was in a terrarium, and only about 18 inches long, but hey, it was a croc! Now you might expect to see a guy with a pet croc in Australia, or maybe in the Bayou, but in Seattle? Hmm. Among the other interesting customers on my route, was Miss Teenage Seattle. She and her sisters were both models and beauty contestants. Conveniently, their neighbor was a professional photographer (a woman). The photographer was also a customer of mine, so I saw some of the pictures of the photo-shoots. No, there was nothing risqué or inappropriate. Just a posed girl, fully and properly clothed. Being pretty shy, I asked if I could have a copy of one of them (because the girl was famous). The photographer got permission from the girl and then gave me a little 2 x 2 photo proof, which I kept in my wallet until I lost it a few months later. There were other oddities and beautiful people on my route, but those little tidbits can wait for another day.

Okay, our little break is over, so let's get to work on what is really important.

Some Other Parables

Before we move on to the more direct information that Jesus gave his disciples about their future, I think we need to briefly look at other parables so we can compare their messages. Case in point, if what Jesus said was consistent, then we get a better idea of what he truly said about events that were to happen later. One passage or one parable could be misinterpreted, but if many different lessons say the same thing from different angles, then we can more easily detect the overlaps that reinforce the real truth.

A Lot of Fish

The next prophetic parable we can discuss is the lesson of "The Net." We find it in Matthew 13:47-50.

> **"Once again, the kingdom of heaven is like a net that was let down into the lake and caught all kinds of fish. When it was full, the fishermen pulled it up on the shore. Then they sat down and collected the good fish in baskets, but threw the bad away. This is how it will be at the end of the age. The angels will come and separate the wicked from the righteous and throw them into the blazing furnace, where there will be weeping and gnashing of teeth.**

Do you see any similarities between this parable and the one we previously discussed? It seems to me that in both parables, objects are meant to represent a large group of people that include both the "bad" and the "good." In the former parable, people were represented by plants (wheat and weeds). In this parable, people are represented by fish. In the former parable, the farmer waited until the plants were mature. In other words, we could say the wheat and weeds became as ripe and as large as they were going to get. In one sense, we could say that for the farmer, waiting any longer to destroy the weeds or to save the wheat, was useless. There would be no gain in waiting longer, and in fact, the best time for saving the wheat was at its peak. In this parable of the net, the peak time seems to be when the net was full. Surely, waiting for the net to have more fish would risk breaking the net and all of the fish could be lost. In comparison, it seems to me that the person who is in charge of each of these operations (harvest and fishing), must decide when the optimum time is for doing away with the "bad apples," and saving the good apples. So, in a simple and Fresh Read, this is what I see (without bringing in outside influence):

Let's focus now on the prophetic part of this parable. The last part of this parable says,

> **"This is how it will be at the end of the age.**
> **The angels will come and separate the wicked**
> **from the righteous and throw them into the**
> **blazing furnace, where there will be weeping**
> **and gnashing of teeth."**

Can you see any common wording or theme in the concluding part of this parable? Well, in the NIV version anyway, the wording is the same. So, it seems Jesus' point was the same, just the objects used to teach the lesson were changed. What is the central point, again? It seems to me that the people who Jesus called "wicked" will be either punished or destroyed. There also seems to be a lot of sorrow and/or misery connected with this process. There is "weeping and gnashing of teeth." So what I get is that there is a lot of crying going on. I am not exactly sure of what this gnashing of teeth is, so my best course would be to look it up in Greek to see if there are any clues.

I will look this one up for you as an example, but this is not a spoon-feed type of book, so in many cases, when we come across words that need definition, you will need to stop and look them up yourself. The Greek word for gnashing sounds like "brygmos." It represents extreme anguish and despair. It can also include resulting actions, such as snarling or growling. Now, when I see this, I am thinking that this weeping and gnashing of teeth, may not always be a result of feeling sorry for what they did. It could just as easily be sorrow about the severity of their punishment. And, this gnashing of teeth could include angry outcries against God for what he is doing to them. Now, I am saying this as a "maybe," not a "must be." You will need to look at the Greek definitions and see what you think.

As a side-note about looking up Greek words, there is currently a pretty good Bible tool online (which also has a phone app), called "Blue Letter Bible." No, I have not talked to them, nor do I get anything from telling you about the tool. I use it right now and probably will until I find one I like better. I have also used Bible Gateway online and still do. There are also several online Greek word dictionaries and Word Expository (e.g., W.E. Vine). There are many tools out there to help, but in all fairness, if you are using these "free" tools, I recommend supporting the organizations that make them.

It is all about the Wine

Time to look at a few other parables. There is one about a vineyard that is worth noting. There are versions of this parable in Matthew 21:33-44 and Mark 12:1-12. For the sake of space and time, I will show a shortened version of this parable here.

From Matthew 21:33-44

> **"Listen to another parable. There was a landowner who planted a vineyard and put a wall around it and dug a wine press in it, and built a tower, and rented it out to vine-growers and went on a journey. When the harvest time approached, he sent his slaves to the vine-growers to receive his produce. The vine-growers took his slaves and beat one, and killed another, and stoned a third."**

This is the basics of the story as I see it: A land-lord created a vineyard, with everything needed to make wine. He rented it out and then went on vacation (or maybe a business trip). When the grapes were getting close to being ripe, he sent some of his men to get a portion of the grapes (or maybe wine). This was likely the payment for "renting" the vineyard. However, if you read the rest of the story in the Bible, it seems the renters had no intention of paying any rent and were willing to kill the owner's son in an attempt to take the vineyard away from its rightful owner. This is what Jesus said toward the end of this parable (Matthew 21:40-44)

> **"Therefore, when the owner of the vineyard comes, what will he do to those tenants? He will bring those wretches to a wretched end,"**

they replied, "and he will rent the vineyard to other tenants, who will give him his share of the crop at harvest time." Jesus said to them, "Have you never read in the Scriptures: 'The stone the builders rejected has become the cornerstone; the Lord has done this, and it is marvelous in our eyes'? "Therefore I tell you that the kingdom of God will be taken away from you and given to a people who will produce its fruit. Anyone who falls on this stone will be broken to pieces; anyone on whom it falls will be crushed."

It seems there is a little different idea here than with the previous parables. What I get is that there is a field or a place where crops are produced and that it belongs to a powerful master, who has a son. I suppose we could assign this meaning to many things or personalities, but the obvious one to me is God. I think this land owner is God and the son in this parable is none other than Jesus. The biggest question I have is, what is this land? Is it the whole earth, or the land of Judah? Is it even a physical land, or a spiritual/metaphoric land? This does not seem to be very clear to me. One clue might be that at other times, Jesus did say being a blood descendent of Abraham didn't make a person a true son of Abraham. Note the following:

John 8:39-41

"Abraham is our father," they answered. "If you were Abraham's children," said Jesus, "then you would do what Abraham did. As it

> **is, you are looking for a way to kill me, a man**
> **who has told you the truth that I heard from**
> **God. Abraham did not do such things. You**
> **are doing the works of your own father."**

In addition, this is what John the Baptist said in Matthew 3:7-9:

> **But when he saw many of the Pharisees and**
> **Sadducees coming to where he was baptizing,**
> **he said to them: "You brood of vipers! Who**
> **warned you to flee from the coming wrath?**
> **Produce fruit in keeping with repentance.**
> **And do not think you can say to yourselves,**
> **'We have Abraham as our father.' I tell you**
> **that out of these stones God can raise up**
> **children for Abraham.**

To add to this puzzle, Paul wrote this in Galatians 3:29:

> **If you belong to Christ, then you are**
> **Abraham's seed, and heirs according to the**
> **promise.**

We might get the idea from these texts alone that God was saying the Jewish leaders were not faithful and honorable toward the one who truly owned the land of Israel/Judah, and who was the true father of them all (God). If the majority of Judah followed these leaders, then they too were faithless and acted in a wicked way. If this line of reasoning is right, then it seems John the Baptist and Jesus both were saying that the land or something that identified the children of Abraham was going to change ownership. Paul's statement also might suggest that all believers in Christ, regardless of their blood-line were considered Abraham's seed, in God's eyes.

Let me say at this point that the prophecy aspect of these verses is highly controversial. Was Israel and/or Jerusalem going to change ownership? In the New Covenant, was the church going to take the place of Israel as God's bride? These and many more questions are debated daily. One thing seems to be clear from a Fresh Read of these parables: Jesus and John the Baptist warned that a change was coming if the people did not alter their wicked practices, and the main targets for this warning were the leaders of Judah. The chief priests, law givers, and likely the whole Sanhedrin were being held responsible for the spiritual state of the Jews. I would say that at the very least, God was going to change the leadership. However, since this whole thing can be debated, you will need to do your duty and study all the other Bible texts that talk about this change so you can form a wise opinion.

Fig, Figs, Figs

Time to talk about figs. Big mystery at this point, right? Well, it seems that these seedy, sticky little fruits carry some pretty significant symbolism in prophetic passages – or at least their trees do. Remember the fig tree that Jesus cursed (Matthew 21 & Mark 11)? Many scholars see the tree as a symbol of the Jewish nation (reference Jeremiah 8:13 & Hosea 9:10), and its punishment as a result of not allowing Christ to gather them as tender chicks under his wings and protect them. However, rather than focusing on this particular tree that may or may not be a symbol of Judah, let's look at a parable, that Jesus told,

about another fig tree. It is found in Matthew 24:32-35 &
Mark 13:28-33 (both NIV).

> **"Now learn this lesson from the fig tree: As
> soon as its twigs get tender and its leaves
> come out, you know that summer is near.
> Even so, when you see all these things, you
> know that it is near, right at the door. Truly
> I tell you, this generation will certainly not
> pass away until all these things have
> happened. Heaven and earth will pass away,
> but my words will never pass away."**

It seems to me, the word illustration here is pretty simple and
easy to understand. From my perspective, living in
Northwestern America, I relate to this story when I see buds
and leaves begin to show on trees in the springtime. Though
the trees are not fully foliaged, I would know that summer is
coming soon. Though I have not seen any fig trees in our area,
I am pretty sure this principle applies to them as well, and that
this same principle applies to most of the world.

Now, what do you suppose Jesus was talking about here? He
said, "… when you see all these things." What things? To
know this, we need to look at the verses right before this
parable. From what I read, it sounds like from the first of
chapter 24, Jesus is telling the disciples about many things that
were going to happen at a later time. The burning question in
the disciples' minds probably was the same as we would have if
we were there: When? In this parable, Jesus says,

> **"Even so, when you see all these things, you
> know that it is near, right at the door."**

Okay, okay - we just opened the biggest can of worms that exist in prophecies. Many scholars hold to a doctrine that says at least some of the things Jesus said in the early part of chapter 24 have not yet happened. So, let me ask you this question: Based just on this text alone, what is the meaning you would get if you read it the first time, without any outside influence? Now, you are welcome to interpret this any way you want, as long as you can solidly backup your claims - without manipulating scripture or taking it out of context. And, I also need to point out that just because a prophecy is fulfilled does not mean it cannot be fulfilled again. Some prophecies were already fulfilled twice. For our "Fresh-Read" of this passage, however, it appears to me that Jesus is pretty clear about the timeframe of some big event that was going to happen, and what the disciples should do about it. He told them (not us), that when they saw certain things happen, they would know that this big event was near – in fact, it was "right at the door." This strongly suggests that the event was something the disciples would see. So, what else does Jesus say at the end of this parable?

> **"Even so, when you see all these things, you know that it is near, right at the door. Truly I tell you, this generation will certainly not pass away until all these things have happened. Heaven and earth will pass away, but my words will never pass away."**

Here we seem to have even more emphasis on the time frame. This could be because the disciples had asked Jesus about when these things were going to take place. As we said, Jesus didn't tell them a date and time, instead, he told them to watch for certain signs and when they saw them, they would know the time was going to be right away. In fact, he followed up by saying that their generation would not pass until all these things would happen. So, I would conclude that everything Jesus told them was going to happen (in the early part of Matthew 24), was going to happen in their lifetime.

Now, many scholars look at the Greek word for "generation" and say it can also mean "race." So, the argument is that Jesus meant the Jewish race would not pass away until all these things happened. If you feel this is correct, and you have good scriptural ground to stand on, great. Go for it. But, in this First-Time, Fresh-Read we are doing of this text, it is hard to see how this fits with the other things Jesus says in this passage. It is also important to know, without manipulating the text, that in Greek (as with other languages) a word's meaning is dependent on the context it is used in. Thus, in context, if Jesus first says, the signs indicate things are going to happen right away (right at the door), then says right after that, the disciples' generation would not pass away until they happen, it seems more congruent. If we make "generation" be "race," it seems to skew Jesus' intended time-frame.

The Virgins

After all of what we discussed about Matthew chapter 24, it is interesting what Jesus says at the beginning of Matthew 25 (1-13).

> **"At that time the kingdom of heaven will be like ten virgins who took their lamps and went out to meet the bridegroom. Five of**

them were foolish and five were wise. The foolish ones took their lamps but did not take any oil with them. The wise ones, however, took oil in jars along with their lamps. The bridegroom was a long time in coming, and they all became drowsy and fell asleep. "At midnight the cry rang out: 'Here's the bridegroom! Come out to meet him!' "Then all the virgins woke up and trimmed their lamps. The foolish ones said to the wise, 'Give us some of your oil; our lamps are going out.' "'No,' they replied, 'there may not be enough for both us and you. Instead, go to those who sell oil and buy some for yourselves.' "But while they were on their way to buy the oil, the bridegroom arrived. The virgins who were ready went in with him to the wedding banquet. And the door was shut. "Later the others also came. 'Lord, Lord,' they said, 'open the door for us!' "But he replied, 'Truly I tell you, I don't know you.' "Therefore keep watch, because you do not know the day or the hour.

So, briefly, this is about ten virgins that went to meet a bridegroom. Five of them brought extra oil, in case there was a delay in his arrival. Five of them just brought enough to last until the expected arrival time. If we do some back-yard psychology here, we might say five of the virgins were practical (or possibly pessimistic) and the other five were foolish (or possibly overly optimistic). Well of course the bride-groom took a little longer than was planned by the virgins, so five of them ran out of oil. In the end, five were able to be with the bridegroom and five were not. What is not clear to me, is if these virgins were supposed to be the wives the bridegroom was marrying or if he was marrying someone else. And, it didn't seem to be the actual marriage ceremony, instead, it seems the bridegroom was coming to the wedding banquet (reception). So, I suppose, unless the wedding ceremony was to be in the same place as the banquet and as part of the banquet, the ceremony of the wedding may have already taken place. Most scholars see this parable with the virgins being guests and not the wives of the bridegroom, but the whole scene is a little foreign to us in today's America and there are just too many details we are not told. The cap to this story is again at the end of the parable - which reads,

> **"The virgins who were ready went in with him to the wedding banquet. And the door was shut. "Later the others also came. 'Lord, Lord,' they said, 'open the door for us!' "But he replied, 'Truly I tell you, I don't know you.' "Therefore keep watch, because you do not know the day or the hour."**

This sounds to me like half of a certain group of people (virgins) were attentive; paying attention, prepared for going the "long haul," determined, and dedicated to making sure they were able to go in with the bridegroom when he came. The other half thought he would come earlier, and so only put out effort for the "short haul." Perhaps this group of people could be represented as the ones that accepted the seed that was sowed, but the cares of life crept in and crowded out the Word they had received from Jesus.

Perhaps the most important lesson here is that there was a time-frame where followers of Christ could enter into what Jesus promised – and after that time-frame, they could try to get in, but their entry would be refused. Now since this is not all explained, this parable is open to a lot of different interpretations. Because Jesus often targeted the leaders of Judah and laid a lot of responsibility on their shoulders, one possible explanation might be that Jesus was trying to point out the time allotted for the Jews to accept him as the Messiah (their bridegroom). The leaders and their followers, who looked to see if the Messiah was coming, and maybe thought at one point it could be Jesus, drew back. Many of Jesus' followers demanded that he rise to power and when he didn't, they stopped following him. Their loyalty ran out, like oil in a lamp. Of course, this analogy does not neatly fit the parallel, and you may have some better ideas about this parable. I just want to caution you here and advise you to use the RID method. When the text does not actually say something, make sure you don't invent it. Don't play God. It may become clearer later when reading other scripture, or it may just remain a mystery. It was likely clearer to the disciples than to us, as well.

Be Ready

Just one last parable to cover, then we can move on to some of the main meat of Jesus' prophetic statements. This one is about being faithful and it is found in Luke 12:40-53:

> **"You too, be ready; for the Son of Man is**
> **coming at an hour that you do not expect."**
> **Peter said, "Lord, are you addressing this**

parable to us, or to everyone else as well?"
And the Lord said, "Who then is the faithful
and sensible steward, whom his master will
put in charge of his servants, to give them
their rations at the proper time?

Similar to the meaning of the parable of the ten virgins, there is an aspect of continuing to be faithful and diligent until the master arrives (or the bridegroom in the former parable). Though Jesus said the events he described, including his return, would happen in their generation, these lessons seem to warn the disciples that it was likely going to take longer than they would like. Now, some scholars take this text and try to apply the delay to a future time that was thousands of years later, but in a Fresh Read of this text, I don't see anything that would suggest that length of time. It doesn't seem sensible that Jesus would give such grave warnings to his disciples so they would anxiously watch every day for these signs, then, in the end, say, oh, you didn't need to do that, because it wasn't going to happen for another 1900 years, anyway. It doesn't seem to fit with the other things Jesus did with his disciples. Of course, there is room for other arguments, so, you read it and see what you think. Apply the RID rules and make sure you stick to just the text on the page – nothing more.

One important thing to note about this parable is that Peter asked,

"Lord, are you addressing this parable to us,
or to everyone else as well?"

Then Jesus said,

"Who then is the faithful and sensible
steward, whom his master will put in charge
of his servants, to give them their rations at
the proper time?"

So, what do you think about Jesus' answer? Was he talking to the disciples or everyone? Who were the stewards of the "food" Jesus had given them? I think we can see that it would not be the Jewish leaders that would be spiritually feeding the followers of Christ, and the common followers would also not be able to provide the food of Jesus' teachings. The ones needing the "rations" were servants of the master, and there were some leaders who were put in charge of them. Peter, of all the disciples, would qualify for the very top of this role in the early church. Again, this is the aspect of the "long haul." When these events happened and when Jesus returned, the church leaders needed to be still there, conscientiously teaching and discipling new believers. Perhaps this is particularly important for Peter because he denied Christ before Christ was crucified - and while Jesus was in the grave, Peter went back to fishing. He didn't go out and teach others what he had been taught. Only after Jesus rose from the dead, and showed himself to his disciples, did they decide to resume the ministry of Christ and truly launch the church.

All this is food for thought and all subject to our RID rules. So, dig into these parables until you are satisfied that you understand the intention of the writer. When you believe you have it down pretty well, then move on to the next subject in this book.

Chapter 3

Meat: The Beginning

Once more, I want to emphasize this: I'm not here to push my views or doctrinal beliefs on you. This book is about exploration. I will tell you what I see in the text and what I don't see. I can be wrong – but probably not all the time. Similarly, I can be right – but probably not all the time.

As I said in my book REVELATION WITHOUT INFLAMMATION, when I go to a new city, I prefer to explore the city on my own. I like many of the interesting facts that tour guides offer, but I prefer to snoop around and see the back streets as well as the popular points of interest. I want to see the ugly as well as the beautiful, and I want to see those small treasures that tour buses never show you. There's something more honest about a self-guided tour than one that is designed to make you feel good about the city. With God's Word, too, we can benefit from experienced guides; but what we need to realize is that the best guides for either a city or the Bible can sometimes get the facts wrong. Other times there are facts that the guides just plain don't know. I think we can agree on this: If we went to Paris, it would not take a guide for us to recognize the Eiffel Tower. Some things are just obvious, even to a novice. This is what is great about God's Word. There are many things God has said that are plain and easy to see. When we see and understand these first, we can better judge the validity of things that are presented by "experts."

Preach it!

There are things Jesus said that seem to be time-sensitive, and these things often trip-up Bible scholars who are trying to make sense of eschatology. Let's look first at two verses in Matthew.

Matthew 10:23

> **"But whenever they persecute you in one city,**
> **flee to the next; for truly I say to you, you will**
> **not finish going through the cities of Israel**
> **until the Son of Man comes."**

Matthew 24:14

> **"This gospel of the kingdom shall be**
> **preached in the whole world as a testimony to**
> **all the nations, and then the end will come."**

Before we jump into these, I think it is important to point out that in eschatology, these verses are sometimes seen as separate prophecies, thus, they are not required to be the same idea or time-frame. In all fairness, if we read the book of Matthew in the way we read any other literature, we do see these verses separately. Since one is in the tenth chapter, we might not even remember it by the time we got to the twenty-fourth chapter. So, when we talk about these verses you are perfectly right to separate the ideas. However, for this book, I want to talk about the subject matter of these verses. Listing them together is just more for convenience than eschatological accuracy.

Now, as you read these verses (separately or together), how would you interpret them – if this was the first time you saw them? Is there anything odd about them? Are there words or phrases that seem odd?   I don't see strange symbolism or odd phrasing, so I think I can skip the "I" in our RID rules. The first thing I see in Matthew 10:23 is that Jesus is telling the disciples they are going to be persecuted. I am going to stop myself right here and contemplate this. Historically, were the disciples persecuted after Jesus ascended? Yes, absolutely. So we know what Jesus said came true and we know about the time-frame when it happened.

The next part of Matthew 10:23 is tricky to some scholars but does not need to be. Let's just see what it says without any fancy footwork.

> **"… you will not finish going through the cities of Israel until the Son of Man comes."**

There is a big mystery here, right? I mean all the eschatology experts need to fight over the meaning of this short passage, right? Hmm. Well, I am not sure what you get from this text, but it seems pretty clear to me. Jesus seems to be saying that the disciples are going to obey his command to go out and spread the Good News through all the cities of Israel, and yet,

they will not complete the task before Jesus returns. What?
Wait. Does this sound like Jesus is going to delay thousands of
years? Hmm. But, even if I have doubts about how this could
be true, I have to admit that the text itself seems to be pretty
clear. I guess the big question here is more mathematical. Can
we calculate how much time it would take for 12 or more
people to preach the Good News to all of the major cities of
Israel? Even on foot, maybe a few years? I did notice one
thing here that Jesus does not say. He didn't say that the Good
News would necessarily be heard by every living soul by the
time he returned. Jesus only said that the disciples would go
through the cities of Israel, preaching the Good News.

I want to emphasize this again, as I did in my other book:
Whether we are comfortable or not with what we read in the
Bible, we need to protect its integrity by not changing what it
says. If this twenty-third verse says that the disciples would
not completely evangelize Israel before he returned, then that is
what Jesus meant. He would not lie. Exactly how he
accomplished this may be a mystery to many scholars, but we
cannot escape a difficult piece of the Bible by changing what it
says to meet our predetermined doctrine. Either Jesus said this
and meant it, or he didn't. The worst thing we can do is violate
the "D" in our RID rules and play God. If we act like we are
God and overrule what is written in his Word, we become
irresponsible in protecting one of the most sacred things on this
planet. Again, we must read what is on the page and interpret
it without manipulation.

Now, let's look at the other verse.

Matthew 24:14

**"This gospel of the kingdom shall be
preached in the whole world as a testimony to
all the nations, and then the end will come."**

First things, first: Does this verse say the same thing as the
previous verse? I am going to say, no. The verse in chapter
10, talks about preaching the Good News to the cities of Israel,
and this verse talks about preaching to the whole world. Now,
I have a real problem here. The same writer has recorded that
Jesus said the disciples would not finish preaching to all of
Israel before his return, yet here Matthew records Jesus as
saying that the Good News will be preached in the "whole
world" before the "end" comes. What do you think about this?
Let me share this thought: Since I said we could use
mathematics to calculate how long it would take to evangelize
Israel, let's do some math for how long it takes to evangelize
the world. Wow. It sounds daunting, doesn't it? But, one
thing we can do is combine tasks. What if Israel was being
preached to at the same time as the rest of the world? The
math results would be slightly different. Now, let's consider
something else. Let's keep this whole situation in context.
Jesus is talking to the disciples about the "world." Jesus knew
how they received what he said, right? Yes, he did. So, when
the disciples and their friends talked about "the world," did
they think about America? Absolutely not. They did not know
about the Americas (north or south). Generally speaking, the
regions outside the known civilized world were not considered
(at that time and in that culture), to be part of "the world." So,
if Jesus was meaning the "known civilized world," the task
would be reasonable to what Jesus' followers could do. They
started with about 120 believers, according to the first chapter
of Acts, and then by the end of Chapter 2, there were 3000

more. Persecution came later and it forced the Christians to leave Jerusalem and even Judea. So, they spread out and carried the Good News to extended regions. Also, it is a historical fact that the Apostle Thomas followed the oriental trade routes down into the China region. He planted churches all along that route and many are still there (or at least the evidence of their existence). In fact, with the work of Paul, and so many other missionary workers, the Good News was spread to all the major regions of the known civilized world within the first century. It took a lot of people, but with each convert, the task became easier. So, without manipulating Matthew 24:14, is it possible that both of these tasks, Israel and the world, could have been fulfilled by the time Jesus said he would return? It is an interesting question and not easy to answer, regardless of your end-time view. Even if we can rightfully say that this is possible, we have an even larger issue to address. What does "the end" mean? Is this the same event as Jesus' return? It could be and in fact, there are some suggestions in scripture that the disciples believed so. But does the text in either of these verses or the parables we looked at, demand that "the end" is the same event as Jesus' return? Hmm. I would say no. It is possible, but not demanded.

Because there is much controversy over what "the end" means in any scripture, let's take a closer look at this – but let's first look at this verse again.

Matthew 24:14

> **"This gospel of the kingdom shall be preached in the whole world as a testimony to all the nations, and then the end will come."**

If we focus on the phrase, "the end will come," I am going to assume the "will" means that it will wait until the preaching is completed (or God says, okay you got it covered). When you look at this you may see it differently, of course.

Time to engage the "I" in RID "The end" is an odd phrase. Not because the words are unfamiliar in our current terms, but because it is not well defined in these verses. When common phrases are not defined like this, it can be because the speaker knows his listeners understand the terms he is using. So, we will need to look elsewhere in the Bible to see what Jesus is talking about. We may even find other verses in Matthew that define this phrase. I suggest you do a digital search of the Bible and see where "the end" occurs. There may be many, so you may need to weed out the ones that do not apply to end-times.

Here is a little tidbit you might find interesting: As I am writing this book, I am also doing research. So, I stopped my writing between the last paragraph and this one to do a digital search of the Bible (NIV) for the phrase "the end." As I suspected, the search produced a lot of results. In fact, 166 places in the Bible use this phrase. Let me share a few with you. The first is in Genesis 8:33 and it has to do with the flood.

1. Genesis 8:3 "The water receded steadily from the earth. At the end of the hundred and fifty days the water had gone down …"

2. Exodus 23:16 - "At the end of the 430 years, to the very day, all the Lord's divisions left Egypt."

3. 1 Kings 8:10 - At the end of twenty years, during which Solomon built these two buildings—the temple of the Lord and the royal palace –

4. 2 Kings 24:20 - It was because of the Lord's anger that all this happened to Jerusalem and Judah, and in the end he thrust them from his presence.

5. Matthew 13:39-40 --- and the enemy who sows them is the devil. The harvest is the end of the age, and the harvesters are angels.

6. Matthew 13:49 - This is how it will be at the end of the age. The angels will come and separate the wicked from the righteous.

7. Matthew 24:3 (same chapter as the verse we are studying) - As Jesus was sitting on the Mount of Olives, the disciples came to him privately. "Tell us," they said, "when will this happen, and what will be the sign of your coming and of the end of the age?"

Now that we have some results, let's see how we can apply these verses to our subject verse (Matthew 24:14). As a reminder, we are trying to resolve a problem with Matthew 24:14, that came to light when we applied the "I" in our RID rules. The phrase "the end" did not seem to be well defined, at least within the verse itself. The search we did may bring in other concepts and uses of this phrase in God's Word, thus we may get a better definition of the phrase. So, let's jump into this and see what these sample verses show us.

One thing I noticed in this search is that in most cases it seemed our phrase "the end" was used in connection with a time-frame. This is important as we look at other uses, so file it away in the back of your head. In other cases, our phrase was used for the end of objects. For instance, the end of a garment's tassel or the ends of the earth. The verse in 2 Kings 24:20 may be an exception to these usages, however (see below).

2 Kings 24:20

> **"It was because of the Lord's anger that all this happened to Jerusalem and Judah, and in the end he thrust them from his presence."**

At least in the NIV, it seems this is not time oriented. That is, there are no days, months or years stated. This is not something that God said is going to happen in a certain month of the year. It seems to say that "the end" is when God completes what he had planned. This idea is likely another key in deciphering what Jesus meant by "the end." So, let's also file this idea away for later use.

Perhaps one of the most significant verses in our search is in Matthew 13.

Matthew 13:39-40

> **"… and the enemy who sows them is the devil. The harvest is the end of the age, and the harvesters are angels."**

Does this sound familiar? It is part of Jesus' explanation of a parable we studied earlier. Remember the story about the good seed (wheat) and the bad seed (weeds)? In the passage listed above, Jesus said that the harvest of both the wheat and the weeds, is "the end" of the age, and he said those who do the harvesting are the angels (not us). This seems like a pretty good definition, but our phrase is connected with another term, "end of the age." The verse we are studying does not seem to be connected with this phrase. So, we have another question that might help define our original phrase. When Jesus said, "the end" in Matthew 24:14, was he talking about the same thing as "the end of the age" in Matthew 13? Hmm.

As we explore this idea of "the end" and "the end of the age," we can't ignore the reason why Jesus is talking to his disciples about this subject. If we are doing thorough studies, we need to take all of this into context. For what we started studying (Good News needing to be preached before Jesus' return), we jumped into verses that were part of a much larger discussion. So, let's go back to the beginning of Matthew 24 and try to see the premise for the later verses. Here is Matthew 24:3

> **As Jesus was sitting on the Mount of Olives, the disciples came to him privately. "Tell us," they said, "when will this happen, and what will be the sign of your coming and of the end of the age?"**

Okay, now I got it. The disciples asked Jesus when the things he told them before would happen and added a question about the "end of the age." Now, you need to draw your conclusions about all this, but I am going to say that when Jesus said "the end" later, in verse 14, he was likely referring back to the disciples' question about "the end of the age."

Now that we have some context and some other uses of this phrase in the Bible, we can more easily see that not everywhere in the Bible is the phrase "the end" used the same way. It is possible that even within the New Testament, we may find this same phrase when studying eschatology, and yet the usage may be different. "The end" may not always mean the same thing or the same events. On the flip side, it is also possible that regarding prophetic scriptures in the New Testament, this phrase could always mean the same thing. Study and context will be your friend in sorting it all out. Before we leave the study of this phrase, let me give you what I think may be the clarifying factor.

One thing we have not yet done is to look at the definition of the Greek word(s) used for "the end." Here is what part of what Thayer's Geek Lexicon says:

STRONGS NT 5056: τέλος (telos)

1. End: a) termination, the limit at which a thing ceases to be, (in the Greek writings always of the end of some act or state, but not of the end of a period of time …)

The Greek word sounds like "telos," and as you can see from the definition, it is the termination of an action or event. It seems that one thing it is not is an end of a time period. So, we can rightfully conclude that when Jesus said "the end," in verse 24, he was meaning the culmination of actions. I may be assuming too much here, but I am thinking, based on the context, that these were actions done by either the Apostles (church) or by God – or both.

This seems pretty neatly tied up, but what about the disciples' question? Well, when you go to your Greek word expository (or dictionary), - and, yes, you need to be doing this – you will find that when the disciples asked Jesus about the "end of the age," the Greek word is different. It sounds like "synteleia," and it means completion, consummation, or end. This term could include the end of a time period, but seems to me to include a little broader use - so it could likely mean the completion of actions or the completion of a time period – possibly. If we take another look at this whole picture, we may see indications that the disciples were wanting defined dates and times - or at least the number of months and days. Before Jesus ascended, he did tell the disciples that the dates and times were not going to be told and that he didn't even know. So, again, this text sounds like Jesus' disciples were like us. They desperately wanted to know exactly when bad things were going to happen and when Jesus was returning. If they thought anything like me, they probably thought that if they knew when they could better prepare for it. They couldn't really prepare in a physical sense for what they would experience, and for what was coming to Judea, anyway. So, knowing probably would have just freaked them out. The bottom line is that Jesus talked in terms of the completion of certain necessary things before his return, rather than a passage of time. This seems completely appropriate for a God who is timeless.

Considering the whole picture we have now (or at least the larger canvas) when we study end-times in the Bible, we can remember that the phrase "the end" may not always be referring to the same thing. I think we can rightfully say,

In God's view, the completion of certain things he has planned is more useful as eschatological milestones than dates on the calendar.

Chapter 4

Let Me Be Direct

You might find this idea kind of odd, coming from a pastor, but after many years of ministry, I am amazed at how often people "spiritualize" Biblical text. Why do you suppose so many Christians do this? Here's what I think: We have heard so many lessons on major Bible passages, and so many Spiritual topics, that when we read a Bible verse, we seem to be conditioned to figure out the "deeper meaning. We also seem to be conditioned into connecting verses to everything that sounds similar - whether appropriate or not. When we do this, we eventually view God's Word as a book of principles and sometimes even incantations. We can easily get the idea that if we live by all the Bible's rules and pray or say the right things, we will get what we want. Sounds a bit like witchcraft to me. So, let me say this emphatically: the Bible is all about the author, not about the book. That is, it is not about how well it is phrased and not about certain texts having magical powers.

God's Word is a story. It is an introduction to someone who loves you dearly and wants to establish a close relationship with you. The Bible tells us why God and mankind were separated, and how God took steps to bring the two together again. It also spells out the criteria for each person to participate in this re-union. If you read the Bible this way, then you will get much more from it. And, just to help you see how weird things can get when people spiritualize everything, let me tell you a story about a lady who lived near me.

Lady, Oh, Lady

A man I knew, but was not close friends with, came to me one day and said his wife was having terrible problems, including demonic attacks. He knew I was a young minister and asked me to come to his house, and pray and counsel with her. Having had some battles with dark forces before, I felt it was appropriate for me to visit her. After arriving at their house, this man's wife told me how demonic figures would rush at her in her bedroom and come at her over the foot of her bed. I could imagine her fright over this situation, so I tried to comfort her and encouraged her to use the power she had as a believer to overcome these things. After counsel and prayer, she requested we go through the house and do a kind of exorcism of the house. Not seeing this practice or principle in God's Word, I was not convinced of its value, but to help comfort her, I agreed to visit each room and pray over each part of the house. When it was time for me to leave, she seemed to feel better about the situation and days later her husband thanked me, said it seemed to have helped her, and that she was sleeping better.

Now, this seems like a ministry success and a victory for God's Kingdom, right? Well, it was good work and obviously orchestrated by our Lord, but what I didn't know was that when this troubled woman was looking for help, her situation became known to another woman in the area who was considered by some people to be very spiritual. This other lady, who professed to be a Christian, offered to come and perform a kind of exorcism or purification of the house. She was supposed to be an expert in getting rid of demons, so this troubled lady's husband allowed her to visit. When she came into their house, she went through everything. She looked at patterns on dishes and symbols on boxes. She claimed that a lot of the things in the house had demonic symbols and must be taken out of the house to rid the house of evil. To make a long story shorter, in the end, a whole utility trailer full of stuff went to the dump. Of course, this "spiritual" woman said the stuff that was most deeply evil needed to leave the estate immediately - so the "expert" took those things away in her car. Oddly enough, the "most deeply evil" things were very valuable china and highly prized dolls. The whole scenario seemed quite suspicious.

Okay, I'll admit that most Christians don't go to this extreme, but bad things can happen when we start taking everything in life; every sermon and every phrase in the Bible; and making them more than the writers intended. For example, if God said there was a mountain in the dessert, it very well may be that God's only intention was for us to know that there was an actual physical mountain there and that nothing else was important. Now, concerning this, we do need to ask ourselves this one question: "Are there other places in God's Word where a mountain becomes a lesson?" Sure, that's possible - but when we see a text that says there was a mountain and nothing else is said about that mountain, then we should never jump to the conclusion that the mountain has a deeper meaning. So, as we begin to look at some of the more direct prophetic words of Jesus, we need to keep this principle in mind. Let's try very hard to not put more into the text than is there.

Plunge In

Within the four Gospel books of the Bible, the bulk of Jesus' recorded discussions with his disciples about judgment, troubled times, and his return, are found in Matthew 24, Mark 13, and Luke 21. Since there are many things about the disciples' future in these passages, I think it is prudent we explore them in the same manner as I did with the Book of Revelation. For this, you will need all your study tools handy. When you are fully ready, buckle your belt and put your hat on tightly, because we are going into what many non-Christians view as "la la land."

The first place we are going to land is Matthew, chapter 24. Why? Because I said to myself, why not try to take scripture in the way it is presented in the Bible - Matthew first, Mark second, and Luke third? Let's start at the very beginning of Matthew 24. There are some applicable verses in Matthew 23, but I think we should start where the disciples begin to ask Jesus some important questions about their future.

Matthew 24:1-3

> **Jesus left the temple and was walking away**
> **when his disciples came up to him to call his**

attention to its buildings. 2 "Do you see all these things?" he asked. "Truly I tell you, not one stone here will be left on another; every one will be thrown down." 3 As Jesus was sitting on the Mount of Olives, the disciples came to him privately. "Tell us," they said, "when will this happen, and what will be the sign of your coming and of the end of the age?"

Before we begin to peel open this text, get out your R.I.D tools and place yourself in that mindset. We are going to look at this text like we have never seen it before and we are going to take nothing into this read. Forget the movies, sermons, teaching charts, colorful depictions, graphs, and charts. For now, forget other scriptures that sound similar. We are going to first, just look at the text and take the meaning as we would if we were reading any other literature.

Exploration by Verse Number

1. When I read the first verse, I see that Jesus and his disciples have visited the temple, and now they are walking away from it. As they strolled down the road that lead away from the temple, Jesus' disciples started remarking to him about the temple buildings. Now, what this passage does not include, is exactly what the disciples said about the buildings. The flavor of the conversation does suggest that the disciples' remarks were favorable toward the temple buildings. I suppose it is a spoiler to reveal what is in the Book of Mark, at this point, but it may help us clarify the mood of the disciples by looking at what Mark wrote.

Mark 13:3 - As Jesus was leaving the temple, one of his disciples said to him, "Look, Teacher! What massive stones! What magnificent buildings!"

I would say that in light of this text in Mark, the mood of the disciples was enthusiasm and maybe even excitement. It seems they were awed at the site of the temple. However, I just have to jump in here and ask, why? I am sure the disciples had seen the temple before – and didn't they visit it often? Hmm. I am going to say, no. They probably did not visit often. Remember where Jesus was from, and where he was when he called his disciples? Jesus lived by the Sea (lake) of Galilee, and he was walking along that lake when he called his disciples (at least the first ones). Jesus spent a lot of time, teaching around the area of Galilee. Though people came from far away, Jesus ministered first and foremost in his home region. Even when he was in the southern part of the Judean area, he did not go to Jerusalem that much. Remember, they had to walk to get anywhere, so they didn't go long distances they had to. Since the disciples had not seen the temple all that often in their young lives, they may have been mesmerized by its complexity, size, and beauty. At least this is the way it seems to me.

2. In this second verse, it sounds to me like Jesus becomes kind of a wet blanket on their festive mood. He referenced the things they were marveling about, then said it was true that every stone they saw in those buildings was going to be taken down. At this, perhaps the disciples were aghast because Matthew does not record any remarks being made back to Jesus (at that time). Now, this is not proof that the disciples

said nothing at all. It may be that it was just not noteworthy in the larger aspect of Matthew's story line. Of course, the burning questions you and I might ask are - why and when? So let's move on and see if these questions are addressed, later.

3. In verse 3, it seems that some time has passed. Jesus is now on the Mount of Olives, which is about 0.6 miles (1 km) from the temple mount. Many sources online say it is about a 25-minute walk. So, the disciples had some time to think about what Jesus had said about the temple buildings being destroyed. They may not have wanted to ask him about it, for fear he would tell them more terrible things, but at some point, they got up the courage to ask him about it. Their questions are very important because what Jesus answers is unavoidably dependent on their questions. As we go through Matthew 24, if we cannot remember what Jesus was asked, we will not retain a proper context for what Jesus tells them. So, file these questions away in the back of your mind and keep them handy. Here is what they asked,

> **"Tell us," they said, "when will this happen, and what will be the sign of your coming and of the end of the age?"**

Now, this is crucial: Notice that the disciples asked three different questions. They may have assumed these events were going to happen at the same time, but to break down Jesus' answers, we need to see the disciples' query as three different aspects.

1. When will the temple be destroyed?

2. How will we know you are coming?

3. How will we know when the end of the age is about to occur?

As we go through the rest of Chapter 24, we will need to apply everything that is said to one of these three questions. I can hear those gears turning in your head already, but try to avoid resolving this riddle, at least until we conclude chapter 24.

Okay, let's now apply our R.I.D rules to these first three verses. Were you able to see these like they were fresh and new? If not, try to erase more of what you have heard before and go back and read the words very slowly. After reading these verses, freshly, do you see anything that is odd or weird sounding? Are there any unusual words or phrases? I would answer, no, but if you are wondering at all, look up other verses that use similar terms. Remember, however, that later we are going to go through similar passages in Mark and Luke. Okay, lastly, if there is any mystery here, do not try to fill in the blanks or make up theories to satisfy your feelings of just not knowing all of what is being talked about here. Let's just keep reading and piecing things together until we have a better idea of what this prophetic tapestry looks like. This being said, let's start to look at the next section in this chapter (verscs 4-8).

4 Jesus answered: "Watch out that no one deceives you. 5 For many will come in my name, claiming, 'I am the Messiah,' and will deceive many. 6 You will hear of wars and rumors of wars, but see to it that you are not alarmed. Such things must happen, but the end is still to come. 7 Nation will rise against nation, and kingdom against kingdom.

There will be famines and earthquakes in various places. 8 All these are the beginning of birth pains.

<u>Exploration by Verse Number:</u>

4-5. Diving into the fourth verse, we can see that Jesus first warns his disciples about being deceived by imposters. He tells them that many are going to come and claim they are the chosen one (Messiah). Though there are no details of how these imposters will deceive them, we might deduce that the imposters would have to be pretty good at their deception to deceive people who walked and talked with Jesus for years. One thing we can look at here is historical documents and the writings of Paul (and other Apostles) to see how many false prophets were around in the early church days. We can also see some of the teachings and methods they used to draw people away from the fundamental core of Christianity. Paul seemed to indicate in his letters to the churches that he had some serious conflicts with false teachers for a long time (reference 2 Corinthians 11:1-15).

6. When you read verse 6, what goes through your head? Maybe some movies you have seen? Perhaps some charts or classes you have had on end-times? If there is anything that tries to leak into your reading here, try to put that aside for now and just read the words on the page. In context, Jesus seems to be saying, directly to his disciples, that they will hear news of wars and people will spread rumors about wars. At least this is the way it reads to me. Nowhere in chapter 24 or the surrounding text does Jesus say for the disciples to teach these things to their children or to teach others to teach these things

to the generations to come. What Jesus said in these passages is directed to the disciples. Note that the text actually says "you will hear." So, here is the incredibly large eschatology question: Does the fulfillment of verses 6 and 7 (wars) have to wait 2000 years? Does this interpretation line up with what Jesus said, or is a later time frame for the fulfillment a manipulation of the text? As you can see, a lot of things in eschatology ride on how verses like this are handled. Now, if I put these verses together with some other verses, that suggest a later time fulfillment, then I can take these and say they might be fulfilled again, or I can say that Jesus was just not filling in the gaps and the actual time-frames. I can say he was speaking more in generalities. Thus, a case can be made for a later time frame, when other passages from the Book of Daniel are applied. But should these dots be connected, or should we just take the text as it reads and apply a simple, straightforward meaning? Hmm. This is where you will need to do your due diligence and search scripture for things that properly connect other end-times ideas. Look for areas where war is prophesied and see if any wars fit this description and time frame. If there is nothing that fits well, without reasonable doubt, then I would say, stick with the obvious and simple explanation. You decide for yourself.

One of the interesting things in verse 6, is that after Jesus tells the disciples there will be wars, he says "but see to it that you are not alarmed. Such things must happen, but the end is still to come." It sounds to me that Jesus is trying to console his disciples. He tells them to not be alarmed about the things they hear because they have to take place. In other scriptures, Jesus tells the disciples how to escape the effects of the wars, by fleeing from the troubled places, when they see certain signs.

Thus, it seemed that Jesus was giving them a plan to use when troubled times came. We will look at these things again, later. One thing that comes up again here is the phrase "the end." Since we said that the Greek word for "end" is "talos," we know that Jesus is speaking about the completion of things, rather than the end of a period. Thus, we can know for sure that Jesus is not talking about the end of the world. I am going to say this again: Jesus was not talking about the end of the world! Regardless of what you have seen in movies or heard in lectures, the simple approach to this text is likely the correct one. No matter what view you have decided on for end-times, there is no easy way to turn Jesus' statement into the end of time. It just does not match the original Greek text. It was not the intention of the writer.

7. In verse 7, I see that Jesus said nation will rise against nation. My question here is this: Is this one nation that will rise against another or is this many nations? I also wonder why Jesus adds "kingdom again kingdom." Now yes, I can go look these phrases up in scripture and try to make some conclusions, but then wouldn't that be kind of "spoon feeding" you? Hmm. So, this one is on you. Is there a definitive answer to my questions? Would this be one nation or several? And why kingdoms, too? Now, some clues here: There are many scriptures in the Old Testament that talk about kingdoms. Why? Well, any country that had a king was a "king-domain," right? So there were many kingdoms, even at the time of the Roman Empire. Though the land of Israel was ruled by Rome, The land of Judah still had kings or regional leaders. One of them was King Herod! He was more likely kind of a puppet king, but he did have judicial rule over his territory. Another thing to look at is that the Bible talks about kingdoms that are

not of this world. If Satan and his cohorts rose against God's people, this also could qualify as a kingdom rising against another kingdom. But you can run this all out and see what you think.

The final part of verse 7, talks about famines and earthquakes. I love to play with this one, though I probably should not be so glib. I just can't help but snicker to myself when I see this text used for events that happen in our current time. I can look through 2000 years of history and see terrible earthquakes all over our planet. However, many years later they are mostly forgotten, and then when a new one hits that is quite severe, some eschatologist will speak out and say, "See this bad earthquake? This is the fulfillment of prophecy, thus certain things are going to happen now - or soon." I must say to myself, wow, really? The fact is, there have been floods, earthquakes, and famines, repeatedly for thousands of years. Welcome to planet earth. We don't even have accurate records of so many events that occurred before our modern technological age. The historical records we do have, show that bad "natural" disasters have been taking place, forever. So, this is an area that doomsday theorists can easily use for their purpose. Jesus' words here are so generic that they can be misused and twisted to mean almost anything you want. So, here is what we are going to do in this study: We are going to back away from all the theories and conjectures. Here are the actual words: "There will be famines and earthquakes in various places." Pretty simple, huh? This also seems to be directed to Jesus' disciples, though the language is a little more generic. He did not say, "You will see," he said, "There will be." So I am going to say that the disciples could hear of these things and not see or experience these things, and the prophecies would be satisfied. You make up your own mind on this - based on scripture, of course.

Before we try to bury ourselves in minutiae, let's look at the overarching picture of what Jesus is trying to communicate. Sometimes in eschatology, we need to just back away from it all and look at the larger picture. If we get all the Greek words right and dig into other scriptures to see how they might connect, yet miss the big idea of the writer, we can still misinterpret scripture – especially prophetic scripture. So, I am going to ask this: What is Jesus saying in a larger, inclusive sense? Is the focus in the passage on what some would see as natural disasters? I would say, no. The flow of the text and ideas from verse 6, is that there were going to be big wars. What happens when there is war, especially on a larger scale? What happened in ancient wars that might be a little different today? Well if you look in the history books, you find one fact of war that is not frequently talked about: Famine. In wartime, crops are often destroyed. Even large forests have been cut down during wars. Waters were poisoned, and other horrible things were done. So, since Jesus gave a strong warning about war, then followed immediately with a warning about famine, a first-time reader might see this as part of the same picture and not truly separate events or natural disasters. Okay, you might say, this might be true with the famines, but what about the earthquakes? Well certainly anyone has a right to say these are natural disasters, but there is also another possibility: When huge armies march across a land, especially with heavy artillery equipment, horses, chariots, and supply wagons, it makes the earth quake. In the Greek text, this effect would satisfy the words used by the writer. This quaking in Greek can be from any source. It does not have to be the same definition as our English word, "earthquake." It is literally, a shaking of the ground. So, let's keep this as simple as we can and try to keep things in context, both from a word-to-word point of view and from the larger perspective.

Okay, let's now apply our R.I.D rules to the verses we just discussed. I identified things we needed to look into in each paragraph, but is there anything else you see that is weird? When we do a Fresh Read of these passages, we will likely see them in a different light. This is good, but it also can leave us wondering about the definitions of symbols and terms that we have previously heard. When we remove these ideas (for now), we can be left with things that we need to check out. And if we cannot be sure of ideas of symbols, we need to leave it up to God to show us in our future studies – and if it is never quite clear, we need to accept it as a mystery that God has not chosen to reveal. In this whole mix, I think we do need to remember that the disciple's questions included this: "… the sign of your coming and the end of the age." What Jesus is telling the disciples in Chapter 24 is important for answering these two questions. Jesus is telling them that these things must take place first, before Jesus' "coming" - though at this point it may not be very clear as to what his coming means. Jesus is also telling them what needs to take place first, before the "end of the age." This could be the age of the Roman Rule (in the disciple's thinking), the age of the Jewish people/nation, or several other things. The question might even be a hint that the disciples were thinking that when Jesus returned he would usher in the Messianic era that Jews had been waiting for, for a very long time. They may still have been thinking that Jesus was going to come back, overthrow the Romans by force, set the Jews free, and become their earthly king. Of course, this was not going to happen, because the Jews had rejected him as the Messiah. Jesus would have had to also overthrow all the leaders of Judea, including the priests, givers of the law, scribes, and a majority of the Sanhedrin. However, as Jesus told Pilate, his kingdom was not of this earth. Jesus had intended on ruling over the Jews, as well as the Gentiles, and over all authority on earth, as he was seated on a heavenly throne for all time (in fulfillment of Old Testament prophecy).

Pause for Effect

Sometimes verse-by-verse study can become a bit tedious, so let's break out for a minute and take a look at something I find very interesting. When looking at prophecies in the Bible, it is often helpful to look at the secularly written accounts of events that happened after the prophecies were given. In Jesus' time, there was a fairly accurate and reliable historian whose name was Flavius Josephus. He has a reputation among today's scholars as having been a scoundrel, but a good historian. Many eschatologists know his name and most accept his writings as a good reference for the events in his time. Josephus wrote many volumes, but the most useful for end-times study is titled "THE WARS OF THE JEWS."

In Josephus' Preface, he wrote this:

> **1. Whereas the war which the Jews made with the Romans hath been the greatest of all those, not only that have been in our times, but, in a manner, of those that ever were heard of; both of those wherein cities have**

> **fought against cities, or nations against
> nations;**

Now being the person that Josephus was, I am sure he was not trying to match the words of the Gospel writers, and yet what they recorded about Jesus' words for the disciples' future falls right in line with how Josephus records the events that came long after Jesus had ascended.

There is another passage of Josephus' writings that is also very interesting when compared to some of the verses we have been looking at in Matthew 24.

(Josephus) Book 5, Chapter 5: 22

… I suppose the account of it would seem to be a fable, were it not related by those that saw it, and were not the events that followed it of so considerable a nature as to deserve such signals; for, before sun-setting, chariots and troops of soldiers in their armor were seen running about among the clouds, and surrounding of cities. Moreover, at that feast which we call Pentecost, as the priests were going by night into the inner [court of the temple,] as their custom was, to perform their sacred ministrations, they said that, in the first place, they felt a quaking and heard a great noise, and after that they heard a sound as of a great multitude, saying, "Let us remove hence." …

Now, you can interpret this any way you like, but it seems that what Josephus wrote implies that the army surrounding the cities was heard as a quaking. When I read this, it tends to support the idea that the prophesied earthquake was not a natural event. When the armies rose, nation against nation, the earth shook. Still, there is room for discussion here, so I encourage you to look into the writings of Josephus and any other reliable historians to see if events within the first century after Christ, match with the foretelling of Jesus. If there is a good match, then we cannot ignore it. We can say that the prophecies may be repeated later – and even repeated more than one time, but we cannot completely ignore historical facts if they match Jesus' description of future events (from the disciple's perspective).

Back to Matthew

Time for a fresh cup of coffee, right? Break time!

But, right after we go get the coffee, we must dive into the rest of Matthew 24 – and see it through to the end. Seems like we are approaching a marathon, here. ☺

Let's pick up our study at Matthew 24:8-14.

> **8. "All these are the beginning of birth pains.**
> **9. "Then you will be handed over to be**
> **persecuted and put to death, and you will be**
> **hated by all nations because of me. 10 At**
> **that time many will turn away from the faith**
> **and will betray and hate each other, 11 and**
> **many false prophets will appear and deceive**
> **many people. 12 Because of the increase of**
> **wickedness, the love of most will grow cold,**
> **13 but the one who stands firm to the end will**
> **be saved. 14 And this gospel of the kingdom**
> **will be preached in the whole world as a**

**testimony to all nations, and then the end will
come.**

8. Okay, who is having a baby here? This is odd terminology because there has been no mention of a mother or a pregnancy. So what is Jesus talking about? You might want to look into some other scriptures that use the symbolism of child birth to see if you can get some ideas, but be very careful. Many scholars error when they look for other texts that include the same subject matter and then jump on the first one they come across. We may get some clues on how to interpret one text from another, but let me be very emphatic here:

> **Just because another text or prophecy
> includes a birthing mother, does not mean
> that the two prophecies are about the same
> event! To apply studies in this fashion is
> connecting dots in scripture that authors did
> not necessarily intend!**

So, here is a rule you must adopt if you are going to respect the purity of the text:

> **Unless a writer in the Bible specifically
> references another author in the Bible (e.g.,
> Jesus quoting Isaiah), never arbitrarily
> connect scriptures just because they use the
> same word or symbol.**

If two passages, in context, obviously talk about the same subject, and there is the same phrasing, and talk about the same period, then you can rightfully connect them for study purposes. Even then, any conclusions you make should be based on "this sounds like it could be talking about the same event." When we dogmatically teach or preach our findings, then we can get into a self-feeding spiral of doctrine. When this happens, we build one speculation on another, believing that every step and every level is correct. It is an eschatological house of cards and the whole thing can come tumbling down when challenged apologetically. We know in part, and we will never know in full as long as we are on this planet.

9-14. I am pretty sure that when Jesus began relaying this next part of the disciple's future, they were quite uncomfortable. In verse 9, he seems to say their future was that they would be turned over to those who would persecute them and kill them. I suppose we can assume this process includes some torture and abuse here, but Jesus is not specific about all the things they will experience. Maybe this is the same mannerism God uses across history and for our future. He tells us only what we need to know and keeps back details that would freak us out. His loving nature throughout prophecies seems to veil things we don't need to know and holds back information about the worst horrors. Looking back at this verse, Jesus also adds that the disciples will be hated in every country. Wow. What a legacy to look forward to.

As we look at verse 10, it sounds like Jesus is saying that many of his followers/disciples will abandon Christianity and even turn believers over to the authorities. So, what can you glean from these words? Does this sound like the persecution and executions that begin to take place discourages many Christians, so they "change sides?" I think it is not a stretch of the text to think that some of these ex-Christians turn against those who retain their faith and even assist the authorities in finding them.

In verse 11, Jesus says in this same time-period, many false prophets will show up. Now, Paul talked about preachers who purposely sounded like they were believers in Christ, but were trying to bring trouble to the Christian church. In this text, the situation Jesus is talking about is connected with turning away from faith, and betrayal. When we look at it in this light, we can rightfully conclude that there is a surge in the number of false prophets. If we put ourselves into this period of betrayal, it is not beyond common reasoning to see that if someone wanted to "catch" a Christian, a good method would be to appear as a Christian. And, if you wanted to catch a lot of Christians, you would appear as a Christian teacher.

Now, a common historical interpretation of this passage tends to see the text "will appear and deceive many people" in verse 11, meaning they would perform miracles. This is possible, but if we are observing the "R" in RID, we must keep to the idea of deception, without interjecting other ideas that may or may not fit. If we follow simple common sense here, it is more likely that was is happening is that this "deception" is the ruse of portraying themselves as real prophets, when in fact, they are imposters with nefarious motives.

When we reach verse 12, we see that Jesus extends ideas that are similar to the previous verses. Wickedness will increase and love will fade out. This is often thought of in historical eschatology as a time when a society grows more wicked - but if we read this simply and freshly, we keep these ideas in context with what Jesus just said in the previous verse. This wickedness may very well be the wickedness of followers who turn their backs on Christ and turn against those they formerly treated as brothers. I think we can rightfully interpret this verse as some people pulling away from their faith and others being afraid to identify with Christianity, even if they have not turned away from their belief in Jesus. If we try to take what Jesus said and apply it to other things happening at the time, it may not be wrong, but it is making the text focus on aspects that Jesus is not talking about in these few verses. So, let's try to stay within the scope of what Jesus is saying.

Jesus seems to speak a ray of hope in verse 13, and maybe this is a breath of fresh air for the disciples. Jesus says that the person who stands firm to the end will be saved. Now, I need to ask how you view this verse. The words are simple, but again some details are missing. We don't want to fill in what is not said, but we do want to make sure we reference other things that were said before in this verse. So, what do you think this means? Hmm. The way I look at this is in context with the verse before it. If Jesus just said that many were going to leave the faith and abandon them, then "standing firm" seems to be the rabbinical opposite of that. Rabbis tended to teach in hyperbole and Jesus used this method many times in his teachings. Hyperbole is where you say things as complete opposites to make a point of contrast between ideas. The comparison is often extreme to make sure there is no confusion about how absolute the idea is. If Jesus said that to love him you must hate your mother, his teaching was that the gap between loving him and loving your mother was as wide as love is to hate. He did not mean for people to hate their mother. This was a common rabbinical teaching style. So, in verse 13, along with the previous verses, Jesus may be stating opposites - those who are traitors to the faith and those who stand firm in the faith. Of course, there is room for debate here, so you will need to make up your own mind.

Verse 14 seems to break from the flow of things the disciples will endure, and focus more on their task and their accomplishments. It is not an instruction to go out and preach the Good News, it is a foretelling that the Good News will be preached in the whole world. It seems to me that Jesus is encouraging his disciples here. He is letting them know that through all the persecution and death, their efforts will not be in vain and they will accomplish the task Jesus gave them. He also adds that when that is accomplished, the end will come. Again, this is not an end to a time-frame, by definition of the Greek word. Jesus seems to be saying that once the Good News is preached to all the nations, their tasking is complete. Did Jesus mean there was nothing more to do in Christianity? No more tasks? This was the end of the world? No, I do not see this here. This is a message to the disciples. We can learn things from what Jesus told them, but foremost, Jesus was instructing and encouraging his disciples. It applied first and primarily to them. Keeping this completely in context with the setting, the people, and what Jesus is saying, I am going to say that Jesus is telling them they will be successful in their Christian work, and even though all these terrible things happen, when the Good News is spread, their work will be complete and the terrible events that God ordained will be over. In a sense, and for that era of time, all things that were planned by God will be accomplished.

Let's now review these verses with our RID rules. We tried to look at them fresh and new, without preconceived ideas. Now, we can ask, is there anything weird here? Are there unusual terms? I think we handled the smaller anomalies within the discussion above; terms like "the end" and "stand firm" for instance. If you see anything else in this passage, however, you must search scripture to find other instances where these terms are used. If you can find these terms in the text that is close to where you are reading, it will likely give you better results. When you do find terms in other scripture, always make sure the usage of the term is concerning the same type of situation. If not, then discard that search result. The same term does not guarantee the same contextual meaning. Finally, our "D" in RID means we do not play God. If God's Word is not clear, then leave it as a mystery. God does hide many things on purpose.

Chapter 5

A Change of Method

Okay, I want to change gears here. We have taken much of
Matthew 24, verse by verse, so I think by now, you get the idea
of reading Biblical text for what it says on the page, rather than
the typical theoretic tapestry that is woven with many other
scriptures to form doctrines which may or may not be
applicable. We have discussed how connecting dots from other
texts potentially leads to the creation of new doctrines that
were never intended by the author. I have also shown you how
to look up terms that are odd or unfamiliar. And I have
stressed to not play God when looking at Biblical text.
However, before we jump into our study again, I want to
present a point of interest.

A Friend

I once had a friend who seemed to attract tragedies. There seemed to always be someone dying or becoming very ill. I know some people would claim this is "karma," but I find no basis for "karma" in God's Word. Biblical doctrine, says God is in control and he governs our lives. However, even unbelievers that could claim my friend was drawing the tragedies into their life, seemed to have no case. I never saw anything this person did to deserve or promote tragedies.

What is interesting about people who are constantly surrounded by sorrows, is that if you tell them about some horrible thing in your life, they will always top your tragedy with a recent story of a worse tragedy. Okay, yes, I know tragedies should not be a competition, but I think when anyone is hurting, they need sympathy from friends. If a friend is always going through terrible things, they are just not going to be a good source of comfort.

I suppose when any person is going through multiple tragedies, we could call this era in their life a time of "tribulation." Similarly, any time in history where there was a long period of trouble, could be termed a time of tribulation. Tribulation is native to our planet. However, when one time period for a specific people is particularly terrible, we could say they are experiencing a great tribulation. When we look back at that time period, we may refer to that terrible time as "the great tribulation." Now, I don't think what my friend was experiencing was a great tribulation, but to them, I am sure the frequent sorrow was pretty great.

Is there an overarching lesson here? Maybe. Perhaps the terms we all use are frequently governed by relative perspective. To some people, if events are the worse they have seen or experienced, and they cannot imagine how they could be any worse, then the events are the worst this world has ever seen. So, when we read scripture and God is telling someone about their future, we need to keep in mind that God does deal with us in the frame-work of who we are and how we perceive things. If God didn't care about bending down and dealing with us on our level, then he would not take the time to speak to us in our native language and use phrases we can understand. He wants us to know what he tells us. He is not a God who wastes his own time or ours with gibberish. Thus, we can be pretty sure when God says the sky will be red, it is not a matter of the sky being red to God – it is a matter of the sky being red to the person God is speaking too. If we can see this mannerism of our Lord, then it is not a leap to understand that when Jesus was foretelling the disciples' future, he told them things within the framework of their perception. In other words, the events would be seen by the disciples in the manner Jesus described.

Back to Finding Truth

As I said previously, I am changing gears. From this point on, I am going to back away and try to look at prophetic texts from a higher point of view. I will try to list larger passages and mostly zero in on the high points. The deeper verse-to-verse study is now mostly on your shoulders. When you find more concerning things, you will need to run them out – and I mean purely - not becoming embroiled in "what ifs" or getting burdened down by a hundred intricate theories. This all said, let's look at the next section of Matthew 24.

15 "So when you see standing in the holy place 'the abomination that causes desolation,' spoken of through the prophet Daniel—let the reader understand— 16 then let those who are in Judea flee to the mountains. 17 Let no one on the housetop go down to take anything out of the house. 18 Let no one in the field go back to get their cloak. 19 How dreadful it will be in those days for pregnant women and nursing mothers! 20 Pray that your flight will not take place in winter or on the Sabbath. 21 For then there will be great distress, unequaled from the beginning of the world until now—and never to be equaled again. 22 "If those days had not been cut short, no one would survive, but for the sake of the elect those days will be shortened.

This is a critical portion of scripture and it has been inflamed, twisted, manipulated, and theorized to the maximum. So, for this area and the sections that follow in this chapter, we need to be particularly careful not to interject ideas that are not on the page. The first guard we need to put in place is the one that keeps us from seeing this text as specifically directed to us, 2000 years later. There is no indication I can find in the Apostles' writings that says Jesus' prophetic words were meant for far future generations. If you can find such text and make a good case for it in scripture, I respect your view and will say that you have every right to hold to that belief. As of yet, however, I have just not seen convincing proof.

Now, when we look at this text, what do we see as a simple overview? Maybe I am just a crazy old scholar, but it sounds to me like Jesus was warning his disciples about something very bad that was going to happen. This is described in the NIV Bible as a time of "great distress," but in the old King James Version, the phrasing is like this: "For then shall be great tribulation." I don't want to be guilty of too much editorial at this point, after all, this book is not meant to be a Dave Campbell commentary – however, I think it is important to note that many historical scholars have labeled this terrible event or period as "The Great Tribulation."

If you have been in the Christian church world for very long, you have likely heard the term "Great Tribulation," seen artists' depiction of it, seen charts and graphs about it, and likely have seen and/or heard about movies portraying what this period would be like. Since the water is muddied on this subject, we need to try to get some clarity. In my experience, clarity seems to emerge when we try to remove all the complexities of attached prophetic strings. Some of these strings to other texts and ideas may apply, but some do not. When we are doing a first and Fresh Read of this text, however, we need to drop these strings, at least for now, and simply look at what the Biblical text says, by itself. We can get some very good information here, just by considering what is on the page.

The first thing I think we need to consider is that this description in the KJV, "For then shall be great tribulation," is not a title. Notice that even in the KJV, it is not capitalized. In the NIV and other translations, this period of "great distress," is just that. It is a time-period where there is a tremendous amount of trouble and hardship for people. It is, then, a time when there are great tribulations. There have been many times in history when there was great tribulation on a people and a region. I would say the Second World War was a time of great tribulation for a lot of people. Now Jesus did say this particular time period was going to be unequaled. This could have been a global statement that included stresses for any people on planet earth, but it also could have been about the worst thing that ever happened to the Jews or to that region. When viewing the events, the whole known civilized world may see it as the worst they have seen for those people and that region, but the idea that nothing had ever occurred that bad on planet earth, nor ever was again, is a bit of a stretch of the text in chapter 24 – in my opinion. You read it carefully, go over it, and see what you think. In the end, regardless of how bad this period is, I think we do a disservice to the text to create a period that is labeled "The Great Tribulation." I don't see this as something God has proclaimed. It sounds more like something man has created for convenience or possibly for a little eschatological "hype."

There are a lot of bad things that were going to happen during this troubled time, but of course, the key to Jesus' warning is at the beginning of the section. In verses 15-16, Jesus said,

> **15 "So when you see standing in the holy place 'the abomination that causes desolation,' spoken of through the prophet Daniel—let the reader understand— 16 then let those who are in Judea flee to the mountains.**

Using our R.I.D, we can see something odd here. There is a reference to the "abomination that causes desolation." This phrase is absolutely not something we use in everyday language and it is not talked about throughout the Bible. So, you will need to go and look this up. You will find it in prophecies in the Book of Daniel, 9:27; 11:31; 12:11. Now, scholars do not all agree about what this abomination is, but in a simple take of the texts that talk about it, I think we can rightfully conclude that this involves the desecration of the temple. It is also possible (though it is not absolute), that this desecration may include man setting himself up in the temple as a god.

Here is where things get very sticky in eschatology and prophetic studies. The prophecy of the abomination that causes desolation, was to happen in Daniel's future. However, by Jesus' time, this prophecy was considered fulfilled, in the view of the Jews. Consider this tidbit of Jewish history from the internet (several sources):

> **In 167 B.C. a Greek ruler by the name of Antiochus Epiphanies set up an altar to Zeus over the altar of burnt offerings in the Jewish temple in Jerusalem. He also sacrificed a pig on the altar in the Temple in Jerusalem.**

So, apparently, 167 years before Jesus, the abomination that causes desolation was fulfilled. And, you know what? Any good Bible scholar knows this. The Christian church knows this and accepts this. It is not a secret. What is interesting in Matthew, chapter 24, is that Jesus appears to be saying this is going to occur again. And guess what else? It did. Here is an excerpt from an online source (checked by other sources as well):

> **"Josephus, who was a first-century Jewish eyewitness to the events of AD 66-70, specifically wrote that the "abomination of desolation" was fulfilled both under Antiochus and finally with the fall of Jerusalem in AD 70 (Antiquities of the Jews X.11.7)."**

Other sources (not verified) say that Jewish history tells about the Romans bringing in and setting up their idols in the temple, before or around the time it was destroyed in 70 AD. Probably the gentiles tramping all over the temple was enough to desecrate it, but if they also brought their gods into the temple and worshipped them, it is much worse. The bottom line is the temple was destroyed and there could be no worse desecration than its destruction.

One critical aspect of all this is that by the end of the first century AD, it appears the prophecy Jesus quoted from Daniel, was fulfilled twice. Thus, we can rightfully say that Biblical prophecies can be intended for a future where they repeat. More Bible scholars I have conversed with see this and believe this, regardless of their views on end-times. Thus, as we go forward with our studies, we should keep in mind that many prophecies in the Bible have already been fulfilled. In a wide-scope doctrinal view, it is possible that in one way or another (considering the Spiritual aspect of certain prophetic images), every prophecy of the Bible could have come to pass. Am I saying they have? No. I am saying there are so many views and interpretations of symbolic images and language (for instance in Revelation), that there is room to allow for the fulfillment of things in ways we don't understand. If we do not view all prophecies in an overly literal fashion, it is easier to see how many events from prophecies can be part of our history. And this is okay. We can allow God to be God and keep some things from our understanding – even when they have already passed. The bottom line, however, is if we cannot prove what we suspect, then we do not teach it. If it is not clearly stated on the pages of the Bible, without manipulating the text, then we keep wondering and don't present theories as facts. Okay, back to our study of Matthew 24.

Now that we have established what it is the disciples were supposed to look for, let's talk about what Jesus told them to do once they saw it. In verse 16, Matthew records Jesus as saying this:

"... let those who are in Judea flee to the mountains."

When I read this, it seems pretty straight forward. Jesus has said, to watch for the abomination that causes desolation – or as in some other translations, the "abomination of desolation" (AOD). He said, when you see it, "flee to the mountains."

Here is where I have some burning questions What about those who did not live in Judea? Are they also to flee to the mountains? I would say no, this is not directed to them. So, if this does not apply to anyone outside Judea, then does this apply to America, 2000 years later? Is this a warning to us to watch for the abomination of desolation, then when it happens to flee to the mountains? Be very careful here, because we have to judge the meaning here by just what is on this page. We said prophecies can repeat and they can, but does this seem applicable in any practical sense? First, today we can have no temple desecration because there is no temple. Second, people in North America – or even the vast majority of the world, do not live in Judea. Thus, I say again, who is this prophecy for? Who is it directed to?

<u>A note about the temple</u>

As a sort of interjection here, many eschatologists are teaching that the temple will be rebuilt someday and that it is in this future time-frame this desolation occurs. This doctrine teaches that all the Jews will go back to modern-day Israel and become very spiritual, rebuild the temple and start offering sacrifices again, and somewhere along that way, they (as a whole nation) will eventually come to accept Christ as their Messiah. However, the same doctrine calls for the Beast to war against Israel and destroy it – again. The current issue, however, is that Israel as a nation is not even religious. In fact, from the leaders on down, Israel citizens are very secular-minded. They don't want a temple and they sure don't want to sacrifice animals there. And not every Jew in the world wants to live in Israel. So, in this whole mix and mix-up, good Bible scholars need to take a step back, look at the larger picture, and go back to the actual text. To automatically port the prophecy here into the twenty-first century just does not seem appropriate. There is no precedence for Jesus to warn the disciples to flee to the mountains if he meant for North Americans to flee to the mountains. And there seems to be no real applicable event for Americans to watch for if there is no temple to watch.

All this being said, I suppose one follow-on question has to be something like this: Did the disciples see this happen and what was their response? To help answer this, let me post this (from internet research):

> **"Also of interest, Eusebius (considered the Father of Church History), writing in the fourth century, said that Christians heeded Jesus' warning (Matthew 24:15; Luke 21:21) to flee Jerusalem when they saw it being surrounded by armies. Christians avoided the holocaust slaughter of over a million Jews by the Romans as they followed Jesus' instructions and fled to the mountains of Pella."**

It is an established historical fact that at a specific time, and with extremely little time to respond, the Christians in Jerusalem and Judea saw the events happening the way Jesus had said and escaped the coming holocaust by fleeing to a mountain region (Pella). Thus the prophecy was given - remembered by the disciples and those they told - and action was taken to immediately leave the area. I would call that a completed prophecy. Maybe it could happen again? Maybe, but unlikely – for many more reasons than we can discuss in this book.

Moving Along

As you read further in the chapter (verses 17 to 22), are there any other oddities we need to explore? Certainly, there is a huge urgency in Jesus' words. If I was using more slang language here, I might say Jesus' intention was like this:

When you see these things, get out of Dodge City! (A reference from old western movies).

Jesus was basically saying, don't make any side trips or get distracted. Go immediately, as if the house is burning down. In this kind of mad rush to leave the area, it is not a mystery that Jesus said it was going to be very hard on women who were pregnant or nursing. Jesus also adds the idea that if those troubled days were to last any longer, every single person would die. This suggests that there were some survivors and history tells us that there were – but not many. Jesus also says that the reason some are spared (the time shorted), was to grant a favor to the believers.

More

Let now look at verses 23-31

23 At that time if anyone says to you, 'Look, here is the Messiah!' or, 'There he is!' do not believe it. 24 For false messiahs and false prophets will appear and perform great signs and wonders to deceive, if possible, even the elect. 25 See, I have told you ahead of time. 26 "So if anyone tells you, 'There he is, out in the wilderness,' do not go out; or, 'Here he is, in the inner rooms,' do not believe it. 27 For as lightning that comes from the east is visible even in the west, so will be the coming

**of the Son of Man. 28 Wherever there is a
carcass, there the vultures will gather. 29
"Immediately after the distress of those days
'the sun will be darkened, and the moon will
not give its light; the stars will fall from the
sky, and the heavenly bodies will be shaken.'
30 "Then will appear the sign of the Son of
Man in heaven. And then all the peoples of
the earth will mourn when they see the Son of
Man coming on the clouds of heaven, with
power and great glory. 31 And he will send
his angels with a loud trumpet call, and they
will gather his elect from the four winds,
from one end of the heavens to the other.**

Oh, there is a lot here, isn't there? Now, we really need to put up that past-learning filter. This is getting as sticky as the Book of Revelation. First, we have another warning about false Christs. Since this is Jesus' second warning, we can tell that this was going to be a big problem for the disciples and their followers (church). Here the false prophets are said to perform miracles (at least this is the way it sounds). It sounds to me these fake messiahs are so good at faking miracles that even the true believers seem to be seriously tempted to follow them.

Here is something quite important to note about Jesus' warnings: He said that if the disciples are told, Jesus or "the messiah" is over in another town, or preaching out in the wilderness, they were not to go running to see if it was true. Jesus proclaimed that when he returned, he would come like this:

**"as lightning that comes from the east is
visible even in the west,"**

This opens some doctrinal cans of worms. Historically the
futurist view has been that Jesus was saying he would come
back like a flash of lightning. In other words, he would be here
and gone so fast that no one would see him. In a sense, it
would be a secret coming. Now, if we read the KJV
translation, we might get that idea, but when we look at the
Greek manuscripts, this idea is just not supported. The
language is clear, and it reads closer to what the NIV says.
Using our current terms, we might say it like this:

> **Jesus' return will be so obvious and public,
> that it will be like a huge neon sign. It will be
> like a lightning strike that lights up the entire
> sky, from east to west.**

Notice that Jesus does not say it is going to be a lightning
strike. I don't see that Jesus is saying there would actually be
any lightning involved in his return. It sounds like he is merely
saying it will be like a lightning-lit sky (that is seen by
everyone – even those who pierced him).

So, what else is here? Well, the rabbit hole goes deeper, Alice.
Jesus said some things were going to happen right after the
time of distress (tribulation). This could be right after the
beginning of this stressful time, but it sounds like it is after that
whole time frame. This also gives the Futurists problems,
because they don't agree on how this all transpires, either. It
gets kind of muddy. There may be some clues in Revelation,
so going there and searching for similar time-frames might be
helpful. Reading the first book in this series (REVELATION

WITHOUT INFLAMMATION) also, might bring some light. At any rate, I think it is more important to see what was to happen, rather than try to pin down an exact time - since Jesus didn't give dates.

Jesus said (verse 29)

 Oh, there are so many theories about this text. It will scramble your brain. This definitely falls into the category of the "I" in our RID rules. The question of "If it sounds weird" is a resounding, yes! If I read this for the first time and had no other knowledge, I would be freaking out. The sun will be darkened? The moon disappears? Stars are falling? The planets are being shaken? Just shoot me in the head, right? Wrong! As in Revelation, these are symbols that mean something else. If the sun went dark it would be catastrophic, yet Jesus does not talk about global destruction here. The moon can be hidden, thus not giving its light. This happens from many things, so maybe not so scary. However, are stars falling from the sky? Hmm. Stars are enormous. If we encountered an actual star, the earth would fall into it, not the other way around. Okay, some theorists say these things are not stars, they just look like them – you know, like "falling stars," which are meteorites. Okay, not so scary, unless they are big ones. Again, it does not sound like the earth is going to be destroyed.

Now, if we can put all the conjectures, fears, and theories aside, we can get down to sensible Bible study. Let's go back to this: What does the Bible say? When we see odd things, the first thing we do is search our digital copies of the Bible to find similar language and/or symbols. So you go search and I will go search.

What did you find? Here is something I came across: Genesis 37:5 & 9-10

> **5 Joseph had a dream, and when he told it to his brothers, they hated him all the more. ...**
>
> **9"Listen," he said, "I had another dream, and this time the sun and moon and eleven stars were bowing down to me." 10 When he told his father as well as his brothers, his father rebuked him and said, "What is this dream you had? Will your mother and I and your brothers actually come and bow down to the ground before you?"**

In Joseph's dream, the symbols of the sun, moon, and stars, represent his parents and siblings. If we use this as an example, we might get a different perspective on what Jesus is saying and how his disciples are receiving his words. Since the culture and language were different, the disciples probably interpreted Jesus' warnings differently than you or I would. In terms of Old Testament knowledge (which the disciples had), what Jesus was more likely saying was that this passage was about their leaders (those in authority, like Joseph's parents, were over him), and their brothers and sisters (which would be the Jews as fellow countrymen, as well as blood brothers from Jacob/Israel). Thus, with this understanding, the falling and disturbance (shaking) of all these heavenly bodies, would likely be the downfall of many who were in authority in Judea, as well as any other influential persons they knew. Of course, there is room for discussion and other possibilities, so you will need to look at other texts in God's Word and make up your own mind. For me, when I see that these heavenly bodies are not likely the physical sun, moon, stars, etc., it puts a lot of other things Jesus said, and things in Revelation, into a different light. Prophecies start becoming clearer and more homogenous.

Now down to the 30th verse. Getting tired yet? I am. Time for more coffee and maybe a doughnut. Yum. Hmm, that reminds me that when I flew to Yuma Arizona one time, I noticed the flight tag on my luggage said, "YUM." Can't say it was a tasty place, though - kind of dry and sandy.

Okay, ready to roll?

Let me post the next section we are going to look at again.

> **30 "Then will appear the sign of the Son of Man in heaven. And then all the peoples of the earth will mourn when they see the Son of Man coming on the clouds of heaven, with power and great glory. 31 And he will send his angels with a loud trumpet call, and they will gather his elect from the four winds, from one end of the heavens to the other.**

We have another anomaly here: "the sign of the Son of Man in heaven." First, note that heaven is not capitalized, so this is probably the generic sky, not God's heavenly home. However, we need to figure out this odd term, the sign of the Son of Man – and we need to do this without fancy text manipulations or man-made theories. So, digital searching is on our agenda again. Pull out your digital or online copy of the Bible and search for the entire phrase "sign of the Son of Man." If you are using a different translation than in this book, you will need to search for the exact phrase that is used in your translation.

Well, I am just going to say, hmm. I find no other place in the NIV that has this exact phrase. I find this curious and unexpected. Okay, well rather than trying to find something that sounds like it, and then possibly jam a "square peg in a round hole," I am going to take the simple approach here. I am going to look at the text around this term and see if there is anything that might give me a clue about what Jesus is saying. One thing I noticed about the phrase, sign of the Son of Man, is that "Son of Man" has capital letters. So this is a title, not a description. Thus, we can define who this is by where it is used elsewhere – and if you remember, we talked about this before. Let's look at it again just to make sure it is covered. There are about 186 search results for "son of man," but more of the usage is for the phrase without the capital letters. In the New Testament there are about 82 uses and most, if not all, have capitalization. However, if you look at only five of the search results within just the four Gospel books, it is obvious that Jesus was talking about himself when he uses this phrase. So, we can rightfully say that Jesus is referring to a sign of himself. Yes, okay, some reading scholars, might say, "duh," but I wanted to make this point clear to everyone who is using this book as a study guide.

Defining who this sign is about, still leaves us with the question of what kind of sign it is. So, let's look again at the text that surrounds this phrase for any clues. Notice the very

next sentence in the same verse with "sign of the Son of Man."
It says,

> **"And then all the peoples of the earth will
> mourn when they see the Son of Man coming
> on the clouds of heaven, with power and
> great glory."**

We may be back to "duh" here. The sign of the Son of Man is likely what is said in the same verse. It is probably the Son of Man coming on the clouds. Jesus may be just saying the same thing in a different way or from a different perspective.

Now, you may ask, why did I separate these sentences when we went looking for other places in the Bible with the phrase "sign of the Son of Man." There are two reasons: One, we needed to practice the skill of term searching, and two, I wanted to make a huge point about how a simple Fresh Read can help resolve what seems like a complex problem. Many eschatologists have become so embroiled with individual verses and phrases that they miss the simplicity of what is presented. When phrases remain in context with the rest of the passage, they often become self-defining. Thus, we lose the need for interweaving many other texts that may just muddy the water or worse, twist phrases to meet our doctrinal preferences. Thus, when studying end times, we always need to stick to the RID rules. We need to first, before anything else, read all of the text and try to absorb the intent of the writer. If this still leaves questions, then we search for terms, afterward.

Okay, let's go back to our text and see what else it has to say. I see what seems to be people being very sad when they see

Jesus coming on the clouds of Heaven. First, why would they be sad? I would think they might be surprised, amazed, confused, or maybe just curious – but why sad? Certainly, the followers of Jesus would be glad, right? So, maybe Jesus is not talking about his followers – yet this is all conjecture, not Bible text. In keeping with things Jesus said before this, and after this, it is more likely than not, that Jesus is appearing in the clouds for judgment. This would certainly not make people happy. To give this some meat, we need to zoom forward to Jesus' trial, then scroll back to the Old Testament. I talked about this in my book REVELATION WITHOUT INFLAMMATION, but let's look at it again.

Here is what Jesus said at his trial:

Matthew 26:64

> **You have said so," Jesus replied. "But I say to all of you: From now on you will see the Son of Man sitting at the right hand of the Mighty One and coming on the clouds of heaven."**

Since Jesus said the people at his trial would see him "coming on the clouds of heaven," we can first assume that whatever Jesus is talking about will happen within the lifetime of the same people. The text must be manipulated to make it be anything else. So, no matter how uncomfortable any scholar might be with this idea, this is what the Bible actually says. Even in this light, however, we still may be unsure about this "coming on the clouds of heaven" – which is used in both passages. So, let's go to some older prophecies and see what Jesus is basing this phrase on.

Isaiah 19:1

> **"A prophecy against Egypt: See, the Lord**
> **rides on a swift cloud and is coming to Egypt.**
> **The idols of Egypt tremble before him, and**
> **the hearts of the Egyptians melt with fear."**

This is an Old Testament passage that talks about God's coming judgment on Egypt. See how similar the language is? God is coming on a cloud and the people tremble with fear. In the Book of Revelation, the coming of Jesus includes the phrase "coming with clouds," instead of "coming on the clouds." So we know that the terminology for Jesus coming in judgment can be phrased differently, yet mean the same thing. When we sum this all up, we can say, since Jesus is God, his coming judgment is likely going to be worded similarly to what is in Isaiah. After all, in Matthew 24, Jesus is talking to Jews who knew the Old Testament terms. In our own paraphrase of this text in Chapter 24, it would likely be correct to say something like,

> **"the Lord rides on a swift cloud" – the same**
> **as his Father did with Egypt.**

I think this helps clear up some of the mystery surrounding the phrase about clouds. You can come to your own conclusions and have a right to do so, as long as your scripture base is solid, but I don't think there is a very good case for using the "cloud" aspect of this text as a base for Rapture doctrine. This text seems to lean heavily in the direction of judgment. Now, there may be "salvation" of people later, but, not in these verses, so far.

Moving to the next important thing in this chapter, we come to the angels' involvement. This seems to be something different. Let's review the text in verse 31.

> **"And he will send his angels with a loud trumpet call, and they will gather his elect from the four winds, from one end of the heavens to the other."**

Oh, this is going to be so tempting to run over to futurist doctrine and rapture, and yes there are some verses in Chapter 24 that help give support to this doctrine. And, if you are leaning that way, there is no crime, just make sure to keep the used text in context. However, before we run off in any direction, let's set our pet doctrines aside and just read the text as if we have never seen it - without any preconceived ideas.

When I read this text fresh and new, I see Jesus sending his angels, along with a loud trumpet call. It seems this trumpet call or a similar one is talked about in other places in the New Testament and even Paul mentioned a trumpet call. So, what would be a trumpet call in Biblical terms? Well historically, trumpets were mainly used for two purposes: For direction to soldiers in war, or for calling citizens together. We might note here that they were also used during funerals. The important thing to consider is that the type of trumpet sound was usually known by the listener. Each type meant something different. Because there were no radios or public address systems, leaders needed a method to signal the masses. The way the trumpet was sounded signaled the masses to do certain things. With the military, there were signals to assemble, advance, and retreat. Similarly, in our text, Jesus is either calling his angels to assemble and advance, or to call people together – perhaps both. The text here does not have a lot of detail and bringing in other scriptures probably will not help define this idea. Why? Because what is described is too generic. When we have non-descript phrasing and add other scripture to help clarify, we can marry texts and ideas that may not be part of the idea the writer intended. So, be careful not to go outside the written text, for now. Staying with a simple read here, it sounds like Jesus is having his angels gather the believers together. Since Jesus is coming in judgment, is this to judge them? Not likely. It appears this is a gathering of his elect, before or as a separate act from the judgment. But you can run this all out in your studies and see what you think this text says (without interjecting theories). Regardless of the details of all that is happening here, it appears that Jesus is gathering the believers from a wide area. The text says, the four winds and the far regions of the heavens. Notice heaven is not capitalized, so this is the sky, not God's Heaven home, and not where the deceased believers live.

When viewing this passage, I see no reason to interject ideas from elsewhere about this gathering. I think we should take chapter 24 as a whole picture of what Jesus is communicating and then let the text itself do the talking. If we don't overly spiritualize or glamorize what is happening here, we may be able to get down to the simplicity of what Jesus is trying to say. To do this, let's try to answer this question: Where are the believers at this point? If we go back a little way and use some memory cells, we can answer this. Jesus told the disciples when they were going to see the desecration of the temple they were to flee to the mountains. This fleeing, in historical documents, seemed to be from Jerusalem and the surrounding area of Judea. Now, if we look at this chronologically, we can say that at this point in Jesus' "story," the Jewish believers are in flight from the cities. They are fleeing because the cities are going to experience terrible tribulation and coming judgment. Jesus then is going to come on clouds for judgment, but before or possibly at the beginning of this period, Jesus is going to gather the believers together. Now, notice in this text, there is no talk of gathering believers and taking them to Heaven or the heavens. The language just says the angels are gathering them together. If we look at historical documents, we see that most of the believers, miraculously, ended up in the same place - the Mountains of Pella. Does this satisfy the prophecy of the angels gathering the believers? You will need to see if the text warrants this interpretation and if it is the best, simplest, and most logical fit.

What else is ahead?

We are ready to look at verses 32-35. So, let's see if there is anything new, here.

> **32 "Now learn this lesson from the fig tree: As soon as its twigs get tender and its leaves come out, you know that summer is near. 33 Even so, when you see all these things, you know that it is near, right at the door. 34 Truly I tell you, this generation will certainly not pass away until all these things have happened. 35 Heaven and earth will pass away, but my words will never pass away.**

Does this passage sound familiar? When we were discussing parables in chapter two of this book, I talked about this passage and commented on it. From a parable aspect, I don't think we need to explore this anymore, but I think we do need to consider how this text contextually fits with all of the other things we have been discussing. It seems fairly obvious that Jesus is again talking about how the disciples can recognize the things that will lead up to his return. This "lead up" is not seeing things over several years, decades, or even centuries. Jesus is clearly saying in chapter 24 that when the disciples see the signs, his return is right at the door. And, he said that when they see the signs they are to move immediately and flee to the mountains.

Let's pause again for a minute to ask some important questions. If Bible teachers have proclaimed that in the nineteenth, twentieth, and twenty-first centuries, the signs Jesus described are telling Christians that Jesus' return is imminent, does it fit with what Jesus said in this chapter? Perhaps other texts are better to establish a later coming, but the prophecies and warnings here don't seem to fit a protracted number of signs and then sitting and waiting after the signs appear for years and years to see Jesus' return. It contradicts the language that says it is right at the door, and that people who see the signs are to flee to the mountains, immediately. The warnings seem to include the idea that the people need to flee because there is imminent danger to their physical well-being (not their soul). So, if we are going to be responsible scholars and stay true to Biblical text, we need to look at this and other associated Bible passages and determine the real truth. Now, let's go back to the text and see what Jesus said next.

In verse 34, Jesus makes a remarkable statement, in light of many doctrines taught today. He says, "Truly I tell you, this generation will certainly not pass away until all these things have happened." My question here must be, why does this text have to be manipulated? Isn't it plain and clear? Doesn't it line up with all the other things in this chapter? Jesus clearly said that the disciple's generation would not pass away until all these things happened. Now, as I said before, an explanation that the word "generation" can also be race, is true. This is true with many Greek words and certainly many English words, but when Jesus is clearly warning the disciples that they need to flee to the mountains when they see these things, why would we think that the signs and events would not happen within their generation? Wouldn't the warnings be useless to them?

Now if we pull this to more of the center of all associated doctrines, we need to ask this: Is Jesus coming back to this earth in our future? Is this a Biblical doctrine? Let me say in all fairness, yes, Jesus may come someday to this earth again. Can we support this idea from scripture? Yes, a case can be made. My personal view is that Jesus is God and he can do whatever he wants to do, whenever he wants to do it. Many of the prophetic scriptures could be repeated in the future. However, to twist scripture and say that Jesus never returned in the manner he proclaimed in Matthew 24, would make him a liar. Because Jesus may not have returned in the way many scholars imagine, does not make Jesus a liar. Let's let God be God, and let him fulfill his words the way he sees fit. And by his Holy Name, let us accept his words at face value. If he says certain things are going to happen, and he is going to do certain things, let us believe him and believe in his ability to carry those things out just like he said.

Finally, in this passage, Jesus said (verse 35), "Heaven and earth will pass away, but my words will never pass away." Now, doomsday futurists will claim that this refers to the whole world being burned up (destroyed), and they make movies depicting these events – thus, trying to build credibility for doomsday doctrines. However, to get to the truth, we need to look up the term "heaven and earth" to see if this is the physical sky and earth. If we go there, it does not seem to fit with other things Jesus said. Just as we are pretty sure that actual stars are not going to be impacting earth (because Biblical texts talk about people being on earth after these signs), we can be pretty sure that the term heaven and earth means people or nations that are in power. This is the research you will need to do as a scholar. Without manipulating the text, you need to figure out if this is the actual heavens (sky – not God's home), and the actual physical earth - or if it is a symbol of something else.

Day and Hour

When we get down to the later verses in chapter 24, it sounds like Jesus is starting to wrap things up. Here is the next passage we need to look at:

Matthew 24: 36-44

36 "But about that day or hour no one knows, not even the angels in heaven, nor the Son, but only the Father. 37 As it was in the days of Noah, so it will be at the coming of the Son of Man. 38 For in the days before the flood, people were eating and drinking,

marrying and giving in marriage, up to the day Noah entered the ark; 39 and they knew nothing about what would happen until the flood came and took them all away. That is how it will be at the coming of the Son of Man. 40 Two men will be in the field; one will be taken and the other left. 41 Two women will be grinding with a hand mill; one will be taken and the other left. 42 "Therefore keep watch, because you do not know on what day your Lord will come. 43 But understand this: If the owner of the house had known at what time of night the thief was coming, he would have kept watch and would not have let his house be broken into. 44 So you also must be ready, because the Son of Man will come at an hour when you do not expect him.

Of course, again, there are a million different versions about what this all means, but taking it as a first and Fresh Read, to me it seems pretty straightforward. I don't find much mystery in Jesus' statement that absolutely no one knows the day or the hour of his return (or of any of the associated events). If even the Son of God was not aware, then it seems any speculation of when he was to return would have been quite superfluous. Now, how do you see the first part of this passage? It could be that I am wrong or that I am missing something, so dig and be sure of what you believe. Are there any odd phrases in this part? I don't see any, but if you do, be sure to look up the words/terms in the Greek dictionary, and throughout the Bible to see if you can gain a better meaning.

In the section, does Jesus' comparison to Noah's day seem unusual? Hmm. Noah foretold disaster and then it came – and it was terrible. A time for being saved was given, yet no one heeded the warning. It seems to me that with Jesus' return there is massive judgment and a lot of people perish. Jesus gave a warning ahead of time, yet most of the people who knew about Jesus (tens or hundreds of thousands), did not believe what he said. The interesting thing to me is that there seem to be certain teachers who want to focus on the part of this passage that says, "… people were eating and drinking, marrying and giving in marriage." It has been taught by some (many are futurists), that this behavior is sinful and that Jesus was saying it is not part of looking up and waiting for Jesus to return at any moment. I think if we just read this text straight, however, it seems to say that no one will change their daily routines or plans, just like those in Noah's day. Should they have? It seems to me that before anyone saw the abomination of desolation, there would be no reason to stop normal daily plans. There is no evidence I can find that indicates the disciple's families ceased all marriages or family-making activities. Though Jesus warned this time in their lives would be very hard, they kept doing their normal daily routines. So, preaching doomsday messages that pretty much sound like "Go up in a mountain, look up toward the sky, abandon all or most of normal life, and wait for Jesus' return," is just not appropriate. If after Jesus' grave warning that these terrible things would happen in their generation, the disciples did not go up on a mountain and just sit and wait, then neither should anyone who believes Jesus' prophecies are going to be repeated in our day. There seems to be no precedence.

It seems the verses that follow the ones we just discussed, talk about the same idea as the flood comparison. What I get from this next text is there is a disaster coming and it will be sudden. There will be little to no time to react once it arrives – the same as in the days of the flood. Since Jesus warned his disciples of terrible times, and death – and since Jesus parallels this with the death and destruction of Noah's day, then it seems the context of the two people being together - one is taken and one left, is referencing the same idea. Yes, I know many have taught that the one taken is scooped up into the sky and rescued, but the text does not say anything at all about people being swept away as a method of being saved from death. There is no heavenly get-together I can find here when I just read this text straight. I see believers fleeing to the mountains, but I don't see a mass exodus of all believers, globally, and them floating into the sky. Some other texts in the Bible can suggest this doctrine, but this passage does not reference any such event – at least that I can see. Most rigorous Bible scholars, even many popular dispensationalists who teach Rapture doctrine, still interpret this passage as one person is taken away to be judged, while the other one is left (one dead, one alive). Of course, the cap on this section of chapter 24, may be when Jesus says to the disciples, keep watch. Notice, he didn't say to stop everything else to watch; he just said keep watch. My question to you all is, watch what? A simple answer would be to watch primarily for the desecration of the temple and secondarily for the other things that would happen at that time.

Are We Done Yet?

As much as I would like to be done with chapter 24 and move on, my answer to this question is, no. But, let me take a little pause in text scrutiny to tell you a thing or two.

I live in an area where there is a lot of theft. Our neighborhood is very rural, yet there is chronic mailbox theft, package theft from porches, automobile theft, and even Christmas lawn decoration theft. The odd thing is, the police have a difficult time catching many of the crooks. They snatch things and then speed off. Some are masked, but even those who are not, are not always identified as quickly as people might think. There is widespread fear that in the dark, someone will suddenly enter their property and take what is valuable. There is also some fear that some of these crooks might resort to violence to take certain valuables. As added evidence that this fear is warranted, some houses have been broken into, even during the day. Some people have installed security and video systems and it has helped, but the whole community knows that the very best policy is to be watching and be aware of the danger. I don't think anyone has stopped going to work, school, or any other activity, but while doing their normal things, they are also keenly aware that at any time, something valuable could be taken from them – maybe even a life.

It is pretty easy for me to put this neighborhood idea into the era of the disciples, and maybe even into my future with Christ, depending on how I think about repeated prophecies. Perhaps there are fears in your life that you can relate to when placing yourself into the disciples' shoes. Now, this is not about grasping a doomsday doctrine, it is about imagining the type of watching the disciples practiced, so we do not twist the ideas of the writer in Matthew 24. Now, as you place yourself into their world, let's look at the rest of this chapter.

Matthew 24:43-51 (chapter end)

43 But understand this: If the owner of the house had known at what time of night the thief was coming, he would have kept watch and would not have let his house be broken into. 44 So you also must be ready, because the Son of Man will come at an hour when you do not expect him. 45 "Who then is the faithful and wise servant, whom the master has put in charge of the servants in his household to give them their food at the proper time? 46 It will be good for that servant whose master finds him doing so when he returns. 47 Truly I tell you, he will put him in charge of all his possessions. 48 But suppose that servant is wicked and says to himself, 'My master is staying away a long time,' 49 and he then begins to beat his fellow servants and to eat and drink with drunkards. 50 The master of that servant will come on a day when he does not expect him and at an hour he is not aware of. 51 He will cut him to pieces and assign him a place with the hypocrites, where there will be weeping and gnashing of teeth.

It appears that in this portion of scripture, Jesus turns from talking about what is going to happen, to expressing more of a parallel parable. Unless I am missing something here, however, it sounds like Jesus is still talking in terms of an approaching event that is terrible and what the disciples should be doing up to that time. What do you see here?

My take on this passage is that Jesus is saying something like this: Like people don't know what time a burglar is going to come and pillage their home, so it will be for the disciple's generation. They will not know what hour he is coming. Regardless of how a person may read this passage, the parable or parallel that Jesus used here is only in the context of the thief is a type or symbol of the way that Jesus was coming. Though this is odd, it is undeniable in this passage. I know some teachers will talk about the thief coming to break in at an unexpected time, then immediately switch to Jesus coming to rescue his believers - however, this is an improper reading of the passage and it does not stay true to the original manuscript. By the text and nuances of the language, it is obvious that Jesus is placing himself into the position of one who comes suddenly to disrupt and damage things. His actions are not criminal in a legal sense, but for the people who became the object of Jesus' judgment, I am sure they felt it was a criminal act against them. Thus, Jesus did come to kill and destroy – like a burglar. Again, in this passage, Jesus seems to be warning them to be ready – and I would say that this was a referral back to his instruction to watch for the desecration of the temple.

I agree that there are many pieces to this puzzle, and not everyone will construct a textual picture the same way, but if we stick with just what the words say on the page and treat the information in the same way we would with any other literature, then we will more likely end up closer to what the original writer intended.

Quick Side-Note

You may have noticed that I used the word "puzzle" in the last paragraph. Though this is not particularly noteworthy in itself, I thought you might find it interesting that as I am writing this portion of the book, my wife and I are at the beach, in the wintertime. The ocean view from our motel is pretty. The water is forceful, and the waves are large and frothy. Since it is quite windy and cold outside, I am just holed up here, in a kind of quiet meditation. And, guess what my wife is doing? She is spending time doing one thing she just loves: Putting together a puzzle!   So, I just had to ponder for a minute here about what subconscious influence her activity may be having on the terms I am using. You never know. ☺

Bad Servant

The remainder of chapter 24 deals with a kind of "good servant" versus "bad servant" lesson. It sounds to me like Jesus is telling his disciples how he views the quality of servants. He doesn't seem to say that the disciples are good or bad, and he doesn't say what kind of servants they are going to be at the time of his return. So, it may be a bit of a mystery why Jesus is saying this to his disciples. Perhaps this is more training material for those who were going to be taught by the disciples.

One thing we could consider here is that the disciples did desert Jesus when he was arrested. Peter even denied that he knew Jesus. This abandonment was not only about following Jesus, but they also abandoned all ministry and at least some of them went back to the jobs they had before they were called to follow Jesus. If Jesus had not risen, talked to the disciples, and told them to carry on, it seems they would have disbanded. This may be a reason why Jesus talked to his disciples about the faithful servant and the unfaithful servant.

What about chapter 25?

Yes, what about Matthew, chapter 25? Well, let's talk about it for a few minutes. In this next chapter, Jesus tells a few parables about how people will be judged. Most of the chapter deals with this theme. Historically, most scholars have viewed Chapter 25 as the judgment of souls, after their death, but it also talks in terms of how to escape this judgment. The solution seems to be to obey what Christ was saying while a person is still alive. What Jesus said is somewhat true to all people in all eras of time, but it is primarily applicable to his disciples and their generation.

I encourage you to do the same for chapter 25 as we have done with chapter 24. Just read it straight. Don't interject former beliefs or feelings about the text. If you find odd or unusual terms, search for these terms elsewhere in scripture. It may help to clarify the passage. In the end, if there is missing information or the text is not clear, leave the mystery in God's hands; don't take it into your own hands. Overthinking and overly connecting other Biblical texts can lead to error. My approach to eschatology is this:

Better a mystery than an error.

Chapter 6

Challenge of Comparison

As I am placing pen and ink to paper, so to speak, I am also trying to find a new lawn tractor. I have been looking off and on for over a year because I don't like the prices of new mowers, especially in the class I need. I have some pretty steep hills on my property, so the little boogers have to be pretty gutsy. And it is not just about power, but also about torque, engine durability, efficiency, and other factors. Thus, I am looking for a mower with at least 20HP and with twin cylinders. So, am I picky? I guess you could say I am, but it is because I have seen so many broken riding mowers that were just not built that well. Now, you may have not ever looked at riding mowers or dealt with their differences, but let me tell you, I have run into more challenges trying to compare them than I have ever imagined. At first, even fellow associates said, they are not that much different in reliability, because they all have about the same engines, just different bodies.

Well, guess what? Those statements turned out to be anything but a true assessment of mowers. For one thing, I found that one of the engine brands (for the larger engines) tended to develop cracked blocks. Yikes! Another thing I discovered is that some of the controls for the larger mowers were a little complex and they didn't like to stay adjusted or work right. Now, that is something we all want, right? A fussy piece of equipment that we depend on. Bottom line: I am still looking. In the last week, I did find a nice one at a good price and wanted to get it, but by the time I could arrange to borrow my son-in-law's truck, it was sold. Rats!   Well, the pursuit will go on - but for this lesson, I just wanted to point out that when we try to do a simple comparison of similar items, the task is not always as easy as we might think. So, bear this in mind as we explore Jesus' words a little further.

Where Everyone Has Gone Before

Some of us know the phrase, "where no-one has gone before," but where we are going now, it seems like everyone has gone. Okay, at least any good Bible scholar has gone before. Have I bated you long enough? Well, what we need to look into is, is how Mark and Luke handle the prophetic words of Jesus. The bulk of what Jesus said seems to be recorded in Matthew 24 and some in 25. Thus, we spent a lot of time and page space looking into the meanings (and some lack of details) of what Jesus told his disciples, as it was recorded in Matthew. But, now we need to see how all that compares to what the other Gospel writers penned. One oddity we can note here is that the Apostle John did not record much of what Jesus' prophesied, so we don't need to spend any time looking into the Book of John.

Let's begin by looking at Mark, chapter 13. The first thing to note is that what seems to mostly be contained in the rather long 24th chapter of Matthew, is contained within one chapter in Mark. Let's explore just the first part, first, so the study is not overwhelming.

Mark 13:1-4

> **As Jesus was leaving the temple, one of his disciples said to him, "Look, Teacher! What massive stones! What magnificent buildings!" 2 "Do you see all these great buildings?" replied Jesus. "Not one stone here will be left on another; every one will be thrown down." 3 As Jesus was sitting on the Mount of Olives opposite the temple, Peter, James, John and Andrew asked him privately, 4 "Tell us, when will these things happen? And what will be the sign that they are all about to be fulfilled?"**

As you read this, do you see similarities between these verses and those in Matthew 24? It seems, at least in the NIV, that other than some minor differences, they are pretty much the same. As I read it, the only thing that stands out is that Mark recorded the disciples' inquiry as "Tell us … what will be the sign that they are to be fulfilled," whereas Matthew recorded "Tell us … what will be the sign of your coming and of the end of the age?" There may not be a significant difference between the writer's intentions, but when avid eschatologist get ahold of these verses, they can become walls of contention. For instance, if I just said these things in today's language, with common meaning, they might sound something like this:

1. Mark: What is it that indicates when the things you talked about are going to happen?

2. Matthew: What is it that indicates when you will return and when the current age ends?

Can you see the difference between them, and are these differences important? Well, I am going to say that they could be very important if you are trying to split hairs on doctrinal beliefs. You could omit one of the versions and always quote the other to establish your own pet doctrine. I hate to say this does not happen, but sadly, even well-known ministers and teachers will purposely ignore controversial passages that tend to refute their doctrines. So here is another principle we must cling to if we are going to cling to the purity of the text.

> **We must always fully accommodate every account of a story or prophecy in the Bible. We must not side with one account and suggest that the other accounts could be faulty.**

Now, as far as this business of what the disciples are asking about, we can rightfully sum up what happened (in both accounts), by saying the disciples asked Jesus how they would know foretold events would occur. This covers all of what both writers said, without being picky about how it was said. I think the disciples' agenda was the same, regardless of which way you state it.

Now, since I don't find any odd terms here, I am going to move on. Please feel free to explore the comparison more and make your own conclusions.

Digging in the backhoe, here, we want to look at the next part of Mark 13

Mark 13: 5-8

> **5 Jesus said to them: "Watch out that no one deceives you. 6 Many will come in my name, claiming, 'I am he,' and will deceive many. 7 When you hear of wars and rumors of wars, do not be alarmed. Such things must happen, but the end is still to come. 8 Nation will rise against nation, and kingdom against kingdom. There will be earthquakes in various places, and famines. These are the beginning of birth pains.**

If you are putting in the work, here, you will have your Bibles open to both texts (Matthew and Mark) and compare them sentence-to-sentence. After you do this, I would like to know what you think (though I cannot hear you). When I read these texts, it seems that much of what Mark wrote is pretty much, word-for-word, the same as Matthew 24. Passages like this, lend credibility to the speculation that either Mark or Matthew used the other's text or notes to make their version – or perhaps they both used notes from a third party. It doesn't matter, because all these men were honorable in the early church and their community, so it appears they acted responsibly in their research and also allowed the Holy Spirit to carry them along when they were writing.

The high points in this section include a former point about how Jesus' statement "the end is still to come," refers to the ending of tasks or events, not the end of a time-period. There is foretelling of wars and nations at war, which did come to pass in the first century of the church - and there are prophecies about earthquakes and famines, which seemed to naturally accompany the wars. Of course, you may find other information about this time-period that further clarifies what Mark wrote, so don't be afraid to dig. Just be sure to check and verify the information. Always let the Bible be the best definition of any text before you look at outside sources – and try to stay away from commentaries. They do not agree and they are just opinions. Try to stick with the simple explanation, based on what you actually read on the page.

Okay, let's look at the next passage:

Mark 13:9-13

9 "You must be on your guard. You will be handed over to the local councils and flogged in the synagogues. On account of me you will stand before governors and kings as witnesses to them. 10 And the gospel must first be preached to all nations. 11 Whenever you are arrested and brought to trial, do not worry beforehand about what to say. Just say whatever is given you at the time, for it is not you speaking, but the Holy Spirit. 12 "Brother will betray brother to death, and a father his child. Children will rebel against their parents and have them put to death. 13

Everyone will hate you because of me, but the one who stands firm to the end will be saved.

Take a quick and Fresh Read of this text, and consider what it says – and what it does not. Look for anything that is not clear and straight forward in meaning. Now, what is your impression of this text? To me, it is a warning to the disciples, similar to the one recorded in Matthew. Mark focuses on a different aspect than Matthew in that Matthew wrote "persecuted and put to death," whereas Mark wrote, "flogged." Mark also, at this point, anyway, does not talk about how people will turn away from the faith. It seems to me that Mark emphasizes the spreading of the Good News, more than other things. Mark does include the aspect and role of the Holy Spirit in this whole future scenario. He records Jesus as having said that when the disciples are brought before leaders/rulers that the Holy Spirit will give them what they are to say. Mark indicates that Jesus said it would be the Holy Spirit speaking, not them. This is a powerful and surprising thing and it may have shocked the disciples. After reading the four Gospels many times, I can't recall any place where there was talk of the disciples having the Holy Spirit talk for them, or even through them. Perhaps this is something that was supplied to the disciples as part of the empowering Jesus promised when the Holy Spirit was sent after his ascension (Acts 2).

There is quite a tragic thing described here in verse 12. It is also in Matthew 24, verse 10. Family members betray each other and turn them into the authorities. They even have them killed. So, believers are to be betrayed by even those close to them, and the result could be death. This is interesting since Judas was an integral part of Jesus' followers, yet he betrayed

Jesus and all his fellow disciples. It seems this was a picture and precedence for what was coming in the early church. There is also talk in both of these Bible books about the hatred of Christians by people everywhere.

However, again in the middle of the gloom, there is hope. Mark includes the aspects of Jesus saying, "… the one who stands firm to the end will be saved." Review: The end of what? The end of their task, and /or the end of the events Jesus describes. It will be as long as it takes to complete God's plan. Perhaps this is one aspect Futurists can include in their apologetics approach. If Jesus often uses terms that are not time-oriented, then it allows for more timeless views for prophetic fulfillment. However, if in this timelessness, the tasks or events Jesus describes appear to be completed, then the pendulum swings back to consider at least a first-time fulfillment. Thus, as you read all of these texts and try hard not to manipulate them, you will eventually come to some conclusions that are based on what seems to be the most obvious. The simple answer.

Watch!

As we look further into Mark 13, we again find this aspect of what to watch for.

Mark 13:14-19

> **14 "When you see 'the abomination that causes desolation' standing where it does not belong—let the reader understand—then let those who are in Judea flee to the mountains.**

15 Let no one on the housetop go down or enter the house to take anything out. 16 Let no one in the field go back to get their cloak. 17 How dreadful it will be in those days for pregnant women and nursing mothers! 18 Pray that this will not take place in winter, 19 because those will be days of distress unequaled from the beginning, when God created the world, until now—and never to be equaled again. 20 "If the Lord had not cut short those days, no one would survive. But for the sake of the elect, whom he has chosen, he has shortened them.

From memory of Matthew 24, what did Jesus say for the disciples to watch for? Yes, the "abomination that causes desolation," that was described in the Book of Daniel. This is the desecration of the temple. So Mark also emphases this key Old Testament prophecy that Jesus talks about. This one aspect seems to stick out like a skin sore. It tends to be a hinge for all that followed. Here Jesus is telling his followers to watch for the sign and when they see it, flee the town and go far away, to the mountains (for refuge). After reading this text and the one in Matthew 24, I still see no way to escape the simple meaning of this text, and how it so appropriately applies to the disciples (and their followers).

Now, are there any terms we need to look up in this section? Any we have not talked about before? If there are, go forth and do! I see none that needs attention.

Moving right along, in this comparison, we come to verse 21.

Mark 13:21-27

21 At that time if anyone says to you, 'Look, here is the Messiah!' or, 'Look, there he is!' do not believe it. 22 For false messiahs and false prophets will appear and perform signs and wonders to deceive, if possible, even the elect. 23 So be on your guard; I have told you everything ahead of time. 24 "But in those days, following that distress, "'the sun will be darkened, and the moon will not give its light; 25 the stars will fall from the sky, and the heavenly bodies will be shaken.' 26 "At that time people will see the Son of Man coming in clouds with great power and glory. 27 And he will send his angels and gather his elect from the four winds, from the ends of the earth to the ends of the heavens.

As you read this, you may see the same things I do. Jesus warns of false Messiahs and prophets that will appear after he ascends. Of course, even as it is today, someone is always trying to capitalize on someone else's fame. In the perceived vacuum of power after Christ's crucifixion, there were bound to be opportunists who tried to "pick up" where Jesus left off. Of course, Jesus' foretelling came to pass in vivid color. Many did rise and tried to establish a following that was patterned after Jesus' success. Sadly, a lot of people did follow these false leaders. Some of them had an agenda of raising an army to fight against the Romans, but none succeeded. Even the groups that forwarded the best opposition, were eventually thwarted by the Romans – with great loss of human life (mostly Jews). There were no true successes with any of the false Messiahs in my opinion, whether their goals were Spiritual leadership or military. Each one faded away into a bleak and shadowed history.

When we consider verses 24 through 27, we see these colorful symbols: sun, moon, and stars. There is mention of heavenly bodies, but this could be referring to the sun, moon, and stars also – or it could mean other heavenly bodies, such as planets or asteroids. You will need to do some searching and see if you can discover examples in scripture where these and other similar symbols are used and what they represented. Also, go back and review what I presented for Matthew 24, concerning all these heavenly bodies (sun, moon, stars, etc.). As far as a Fresh Read and a fresh comparison, I see no significant difference between these verses and those that are similar in Matthew 24 (vs 29).

The Isaiah Factor

One aspect we did not discuss when we looked at Matthew 24, is that these heavenly bodies are part of Old Testament passages from the prophet Isaiah. Let's look at these and see how they fit with what Jesus said. And by the way, this is part of our RID methodology, where we look up other scriptures that use similar symbols.

Isaiah 13:9-10;

> **See, the day of the Lord is coming - a cruel**
> **day, with wrath and fierce anger - to make**
> **the land desolate and destroy the sinners**

within it. 10 The stars of heaven and their constellations will not show their light. The rising sun will be darkened and the moon will not give its light.

Of course, I cannot see your face as you are reading this, but I think some readers will have wide eyes and dropped jaws when they see how similar this verse is to what Jesus said. What is astounding to me is that this passage in Isaiah is not a judgment against Israel. It is a judgment against their enemy, Babylon. Now, you need to read all of the judgment on Babylon in this 13th chapter of Isaiah, before you move on in your studies. The wording in the whole chapter closely mirrors the things that Jesus is talking about. When you complete your reading in Isaiah, then go to Revelation and look at what it says there about Babylon (it is a fairly small passage in Revelation). Here is the rub: The things Jesus said, as recorded by Matthew and Mark, also line up with the things presented about Babylon in Revelation. These things that were yet to happen, mirror God's judgment that he already carried out on the original Babylon Empire, hundreds of years before Christ!

Here is something we can consider: If God judged Babylon in a certain way, then later, this same judgment is said to happen again, and a New Babylon can be identified, it is reasonable to say that this New Babylon will be judged in the same way and/or with the same severity. So, the million dollar question is, who was this Babylon at the time of Christ or in the time shortly after Christ? Was it Israel, Judea, Jerusalem, the Roman Empire, the Jewish leaders, the Roman leaders, or Caesar? Or none of these? This has been debated vigorously and still is - daily. There are a lot of scriptures that can be referenced, but if we stick with just what Jesus said, and just the verses he referenced from the Old Testament, we can probably conclude that God's judgment was coming on those who rejected Christ – that is the nation, leaders, and people who rejected him. See what you think, when you run this all out.

There is one other text that Jesus may have been referencing in his statements, and it is in Isaiah 34.

Isaiah 34:1-4

> **Come near, you nations, and listen; pay attention, you peoples! Let the earth hear, and all that is in it, the world, and all that comes out of it! The Lord is angry with all nations; his wrath is on all their armies. He will totally destroy them, he will give them over to slaughter. 3 Their slain will be thrown out, their dead bodies will stink; the mountains will be soaked with their blood. 4 All the stars in the sky will be dissolved and the heavens rolled up like a scroll; all the starry host will fall like withered leaves from the vine, like shriveled figs from the fig tree.**

Again, we see language here that is identical to what Jesus is using. However, in contrast, notice that this passage is directed to all nations, not Babylon (or not just Babylon). So, we might view this as a prophecy against any number of countries or empires. Perhaps Jesus intended to judge both Israel/Judea and the Roman Empire – tough to say for sure.

One important thing in framing the parameters of Jesus' words in Mark 13 (and Matthew 24) is seeing that the words in Isaiah were a foretelling of judgments that happened before Jesus. This is crucial in good eschatology. If the sun was darkened, the moon did not give its light, and the stars fell from the sky, (when God carried out these judgments against ancient Babylon and other ancient nations), and yet the world did not burn up or end, then we cannot conclude that Jesus' was prophesying the end of the world. Regardless of what these symbolic phrases mean to us in today's America, Jesus was not foretelling the end of mankind, the doom of the planet, or anything close to that. If there is any doubt here, go back and read Isaiah 13 and 34 again. Study it closely. The language there seems to be end-of-world talk, yet it was not. It certainly was the end of the world that the Babylonians lived in. Their way of life was destroyed. In our current slang, their whole world was destroyed – but not the planet. Thus, if Jesus used the same phrase and language, the best interpretation we can do is to assign the same respective meaning. Whatever the gauge of judgment was for the nations that were referenced in Isaiah, it must be the same gauge we use for the judgment that Jesus said was coming. In addition, according to what Jesus said, there may be an increase in severity or length of time. This is difficult because of the symbolic language that Jesus uses when describing some things. Please take the time to run all this out to your satisfaction. Gravitate toward simple answers. I think you will not need to go far down any of these research roads to find some answers to any questions you have.

Now, for verses 26 and 27, we have pretty much a repeat of Matthew 24:30. The Son of Man (Jesus) will come in the clouds – and not just float in the clouds, waiting. Verse 26 specifically says that when he comes in the clouds, he will come with great power and glory. In other words, Jesus will be displaying his power and his glory for all to see. You can view this in any number of ways, but in a simple read, this verse sounds to me like Jesus will not be in the role of the slain lamb when he returns. He will show that he is King of Kings and Lord of Lords. How this glory and power are to be displayed is open to much debate, but as a judging king, it is not beyond reason to think that Jesus' return would include a terrible judgment, like those that his Father carried out. We might even consider what Jesus said in the Book of John:

John 5:19

> **Jesus gave them this answer: "Very truly I
> tell you, the Son can do nothing by himself;
> he can do only what he sees his Father doing,
> because whatever the Father does the Son
> also does.**

In today's English, we would say something of this sort: Like Father, like Son. Those that rejected God and ignored his warnings, were judged by God. Thus, those who rejected the Son and ignored his warnings were to be judged by the Son. The only question that remains then is when? We have discussed this and run out some of the probably answers to this question, but for your own faith, you will need to prove these things by a sensible and simple approach to scripture.

Remember,

> **All the best things God offers, are plain to see
> and understand.**

More Figs

We are now coming down to the closing statements of Jesus, as we look at verse 28 and those that follow right after.

Mark 13:28-30

> **28 "Now learn this lesson from the fig tree: As soon as its twigs get tender and its leaves come out, you know that summer is near. 29 Even so, when you see these things happening, you know that it is near, right at the door. 30 Truly I tell you, this generation will certainly not pass away until all these things have happened. 31 Heaven and earth will pass away, but my words will never pass away.**

So, we are back to the fig trees again. Matthew 24:32 to 34 says the same thing. The wording is so close that it is not necessary to discuss it here. As was pointed out before, this close phrasing may be evidence that one writer gained information from another. Though this could be used by unbelievers to criticize the Bible, this sharing of information is a good thing in that it proves the writers agreed on the facts that were presented. Corroboration is a good sign when it comes to historical accuracy.

Now that we have seen there is no new territory, and no difference in the information, we just need to ask if there are any odd terms that we missed when we looked at Mathew 24. I do not see any, but if you do, then do the searches for the terms within the pages of God's Word and make intelligent, yet simple analyses.

The Day and Hour – Again

Let's move this train down the track to the next section.

Mark 13:32-37 (end of chapter)

> **32 "But about that day or hour no one knows, not even the angels in heaven, nor the Son, but only the Father. 33 Be on guard! Be alert! You do not know when that time will come. 34 It is like a man going away: He leaves his house and puts his servants in charge, each with their assigned task, and tells the one at the door to keep watch. 35 "Therefore keep watch because you do not know when the owner of the house will come back—whether in the evening, or at midnight, or when the rooster crows, or at dawn. 36 If he comes suddenly, do not let him find you sleeping. 37 What I say to you, I say to everyone: 'Watch!'"**

Go ahead and read this section, and get an idea of what it says. If you have a good short-term memory, you may not need to go back and forth between the two chapters. You may be able to make a good analysis quickly. At any rate, we need to look at Matthew 24:36 and the verses after it. So compare the text in Matthew, then come back here.

The one thing that seems to be missing here is the part where Matthew records Jesus as having talked about this era of time being like the days of Noah. The whole comparison is missing in Mark. Also, the talk of two people being in a place; one taken and the other left, is not included in Mark. Instead of the Noah-days discourse, Mark talks about the responsibility of the servants to keep doing their assigned tasks, faithfully. At least this is the way I see this on a Fresh Read. This corresponds more with the 45th verse in Matthew.

There are some things Mark records that Matthew does not. This is odd because if there was a sharing of information, then you would expect pretty much all of the text of one would be in the other's writing, yet there are differences in both. This might suggest a third source, but we also can never discount the power of the Holy Spirit. In 1 Corinthians chapter 12, Paul informed the church that God gives miraculous gifts, and among these gifts are divine wisdom, knowledge, and discernment. So it is very much within the doctrines of the Bible to include the possibility of God just telling the writers the facts, leading them to people who knew the facts, and/or reminding them of things they already knew.

The final warning/instruction here in Mark is clear and precise: "Watch!" So, let's review this one more time because as we said, it seems to be a major pivot for events. Again, what were the disciples watching for? Was it for Jesus to swoop down and take them up to Heaven? Is this what the texts in Matthew or Mark actually say? Are the disciples to watch for earthquakes, floods, or famines? Are they to look for wars, the Mark of the Beast, the Anti-Christ, global universal churches, or one world government? How about chips under people's skin? Do you see anything in Matthew or Mark that clearly says these things were what the disciples were intently looking for as a sign? I just don't. Some of these things were to come later, but these were not the sign the disciples were to look for. The sign was the desecration of the temple. When they saw that one important thing, they were to take the action Jesus told them to take. If they remembered, watched, and obeyed, Jesus said they would be saved. This was not a salvation of the soul, but the body. By the clear and clean text of Matthew and Mark, Jesus was talking about saving their physical lives, not their eternal souls. Now, yes, if they rejected Jesus' words because they counted him a fool or a false prophet, then they were not believing in him as their Messiah and savior. Thus, they would also forfeit their souls, along with their lives. However, there were likely some who believed the Christians when they said they needed to flee to the hills that did not believe in Christ as he Son of God. So, there could have been a few people whose lives were saved, yet their souls were still lost; probably not many, but some.

Let me say again, it is important to keep conspiracy and doomsday theories out of your end-times studies. Once you head down that road, it spirals out of control with theories built on more theories, until what you have in the end is very far away from what the Bible writers intended.

We are closer to the truth, the closer we stick to the original manuscript.

Chapter 7

And Compare, We Shall!

One place many people have not been, is sitting with a friend when they are coming down from a very strong dose of an illegal drug. As an outreach pastor, I had interesting experiences when trying to protect addicts from hurting themselves and/or hurting others. Sometimes our ministry was successful and sometimes not. In fact, more than one person met tragic ends, despite our best efforts. As a result of God's grace, most of the people we worked with continued to live on and we continued to help them toward a better walk with God. Though there were success stories, I will never forget the first time I sat with a person who had taken a very strong dose of heroin. Because his tolerance was high from years of drug abuse, a normally fatal level of the drug didn't end his life, but the effect of coming off that level of heroin, with no helping medication, was not healthy nor pretty. It was obvious on more than one occasion that he was capable of ending his own life and also taking others with him. Constant "babysitting" was the answer and though it was tough on him, I'm glad to say that even at the writing of this book, he is still alive and walking planet earth. In fact, a few years later, he did give his heart to Jesus and found a road to sobriety.

You could say that dealing with other people's addictions was a place I had never been to before. However, though the situation I described was an unusual one, I still have difficulty trying to imagine what it was like for the disciples when Jesus was telling them what was going to happen in their future. It certainly was not the projection of a pretty or comfortable life. I think if they had fully understood and believed everything Jesus said, they would have abandoned the faith right there. Think about it: Later, when Jesus was arrested and their lives were in danger, they fled. In these prophecies we are studying, Jesus was saying that a lot of horrible things were going to happen in their region and they were going to be beaten, jailed, and some even killed.

Though you and I cannot fully digest what the disciples were going through, we can try to understand the meat of what Jesus was trying to tell them. With the help of the Holy Spirit, we can unravel things that may seem mysterious from a distance.

Are We Into Luke?

To round out your study of Jesus' prophetic words, you will need to compare what Doctor Luke wrote as well. At this point, anything that sounds the same can bring us to tedium, so, I suggest that you grab a refreshing drink and possibly even a snack. Try not to mess up your paper book, phone, table, or computer while you are doing this. ☺

The area in Luke that seems to mirror what Matthew and Mark wrote is in chapter 21, so let's go there and compare the texts. I am not sure where your head is right now, but what I am looking for is anything different from the other Gospel writers.

Luke 21:1-10

5 Some of his disciples were remarking about how the temple was adorned with beautiful stones and with gifts dedicated to God. But Jesus said, 6 "As for what you see here, the time will come when not one stone will be left on another; every one of them will be thrown down." 7 "Teacher," they asked, "when will these things happen? And what will be the sign that they are about to take place?" 8 He replied: "Watch out that you are not deceived. For many will come in my name, claiming, 'I am he,' and, 'The time is near.' Do not follow them. 9 When you hear of wars and uprisings, do not be frightened. These things must happen first, but the end will not come right away." 10 Then he said to them: "Nation will rise against nation, and kingdom against kingdom. 11 There will be great earthquakes, famines and pestilences in various places, and fearful events and great signs from heaven.

As you read Luke's account, you may notice that his disciples were talking about the beauty of the temple because of its stones and the gifts that people had brought to the temple (likely gifts that were meant to adorn the temple). It seems to me that this is a little more detailed than the other accounts. Matthew and Mark wrote in a little more general terms, whereas Luke is more specific about what the disciples are finding beautiful about the temple. I like this account better, but does this add anything to my faith or provide better clarity to Jesus' prophecies? Hmm. Some may yes, and some may say no. I suppose if I consider the specific beauties of the temple, then its destruction may seem more tragic – thus I am more deeply and emotionally involved in the story.

As with the other texts, Jesus said that all the beautiful stone walls were going to be torn apart – and not carefully. They will be thrown down. As with the other writers' accounts, the disciples ask for signs of when it will happen. Why do you suppose they asked? Is it possible that true to human nature, they thought if they knew when it was coming, they might be able to do something to prevent it?

I don't see anything that is earth-shatteringly different. Do you see any terms we have not yet looked up? Are there any other mysteries in this text? If so, run them out, until you find the answers. For now, I am ready to look at Jesus' response (vs 8-11).

Jesus' Response

Read Luke 8 through 11 and get a feel for what Jesus is saying here. Does this sound familiar? It does to me, however, we need to be very careful when looking at a familiar text. When we dive into eschatology, we will see the same phrases over and over. It is all too easy to allow our natural brain functions to rule over the truth. Every time we read a Biblical text, we need to try to see it in a fresh new light. We may see nothing at all, or maybe the one-hundredth time we come to it, we may read it a little differently.

As a Fresh Read, I see the warning to not be deceived by false prophets and Jesus-mimics. It seems that Luke doesn't use the term "false prophet," he more generically says that many men will claim they are the real Jesus. These men could have tried to present themselves as the resurrected Jesus since the disciples and many others had seen and reported that Jesus was alive after his crucifixion. Other imposters may have presented themselves as the returned Jesus since Jesus had prophesied that he would return. Like some spiritual leaders, today, Jesus' words and actions can be used to forward people's causes. This does not mean that God is in everything they teach or do. Oh, wait, did I start preaching? Hmm. Moving right along, now …

Luke writes similarly to Matthew and Mark, here. There is mention of wars and what the NIV translates as "uprisings." This is interesting to me because there was a major uprising by the Zealots in the Jerusalem/Judea area that caused the Romans to come in and eventually lay siege to Jerusalem, and place rigid restrictions on the surrounding area. I also like the way that Jesus told his disciples to not be afraid. Luke seemed to zero in on how Jesus told of disaster but quickly followed up with a statement that was meant to comfort.

As in other Gospels, Luke writes that Jesus said these things must happen first, but the end (of their tasks or other events), will not come right away. He talks about nations rising against nation – kingdom against kingdom. Since these are a little separated in the sentence structures (unlike Matthew), is it possible that the first reference to war is not the same as "nation will rise against nation?" This is not an easy question to answer, and no I am not going to do your homework for you. You can look up various wars in the Bible text first, then consider what Revelation says, and even look into historical documents (such as those written by Josephus). One little tidbit I might offer, is partly what I said above. The first "war" may have been the uprising of the Zealots as they took control of the Judea area. The "nation against nation," may be a description of the kingdom of Rome, rising against Israel and the Zealots, to take back control of Judea. There is a lot of room for discussion here, and I would advise against becoming too embroiled in these wars. Try to find out the basic facts and then move on. The purpose of Jesus' words was not for his disciples or for us to become experts on ancient wars. Jesus was proclaiming the work of God and his plan. We need to focus on what God was accomplishing, not men.

When we get down to verse 11, we again see the foretelling of earthquakes and famines, but Luke adds pestilence, as well as fearful events and great signs from heaven. There could be some significance here, so it would be prudent for you to search in the Old Testament for other prophecies of pestilence and see if they are connected with war and/or God's judgment. You may see times when pestilence was used as a tool for judgment. As I said, before, the quaking or shaking of the ground and famine are often byproducts or tools of war. One thing to consider is that war produces a lot of dead bodies, and history shows that terrible diseases can arise in an area where there are many dead bodies. Thus, pestilence of various kinds can be part of a war. There are also a lot of flies and other bugs that swarm to areas where dead bodies lay. These also can be considered pestilence.

One difference I can see in chapter 21, is that Luke does not talk about the sun, moon, or stars in the same way that the other two Gospel books do. Early in the chapter, he makes more of a general statement about there being "fearful events and great signs from heaven." Since Luke writes about Jesus saying these things in about the same order or placement as where the sun, moon, and stars statement appears in the other two Gospel books, we are probably fairly safe in thinking that Luke is writing about the same events as Matthew and Mark (just being more general). To be fair, Luke does mention the sun, moon, and stars, later, in verse 25, but this is not in the sequence as it appears in the other two books.

You read the three accounts and see what you think. This is not rocket science and there is no right or wrong answer here. It is a simple comparison of texts to get a better feel for what Jesus was trying to tell his disciples about 2000 years ago.

Prison!

Let's look at the next section, starting with verse 12.

> **12 "But before all this, they will seize you and persecute you. They will hand you over to synagogues and put you in prison, and you**

**will be brought before kings and governors,
and all on account of my name. 13 And so
you will bear testimony to me. 14 But make
up your mind not to worry beforehand how
you will defend yourselves. 15 For I will give
you words and wisdom that none of your
adversaries will be able to resist or
contradict. 16 You will be betrayed even by
parents, brothers and sisters, relatives and
friends, and they will put some of you to
death. 17 Everyone will hate you because of
me. 18 But not a hair of your head will
perish. 19 Stand firm, and you will win life.**

Here we are, reading again. So, what is going through your head at this point? When I read the first part, I see some wording similar to Matthew 24 and Mark 13, but the events are not told in the same order. In Matthew 24:9, for instance, the wording is "then," indicating what comes next. Here in Luke, it seems the same or similar events are said to be before what was said in the previous verses. Why is this important? Because a pure and fresh study, never takes things out of context – which also means, it cannot be taken out of the time-context that is specifically given in scripture. Whether just studying, or widely teaching, we can error in our presentation of end-times, if we focus on Luke as our only text, connect its defined event sequence, and then try to plug it into Revelation to explain John's visionary images, we can get it all wrong. I just cannot stress this enough. Especially in the complex world of eschatology, we must keep things in their proper place and time. We must keep things in a scriptural context at all times, and we must not connect scriptures that are not absolutely and clearly defined as the same subject matter. Just because it sounds similar, does not mean it can be used to define other verses. Be careful, keep it straight, and try to keep it as simple as possible.

In verses 12 through 15, I think you can see how the power of the Holy Spirit is playing an important role in witnessing. The disciples are to be handed over to the authorities, imprisoned, and brought before powerful leaders (likely on trial). In that unique place, they tell these leaders about Jesus, his love, and his sacrifice for their sins. They offer this salvation to the leaders, as well as all those who are listening in the trials. What a wide-spread way to get the message of the Good News out, right? In the absence of radio, television, and the internet, this was probably the most powerful way to spread Jesus' message.

One important thing I noticed in this passage is where Jesus said, the words and the wisdom the Holy Spirit was going to give were going to be irresistible, even for their enemies. At this, I just have to say, wow. No man could do this.

Betrayal!

Now, we explore verses 16-18. We are reading, then looking for simple meanings as well as odd terms. After reading this part (maybe reading it again), what are your first thoughts?

I am seeing the betrayal by trusted people, similar to what is said in Matthew 24:10 and Mark 13:12-13. Though this foretold action is such a tragedy, Luke does not waver from the idea or skip over it. Additionally, the news that everyone will hate the disciples is also the same idea that Matthew and Mark expressed. See what you think, after careful comparison.

When we pick up the reading at verse 18, I see an interesting change in verbiage, when compared to the other two Gospels. Both Matthew and Mark use the phrase "but the one who stands firm to the end will be saved" (13th verse), but Luke writes "But not a hair of your head will perish. Stand firm, and you will win life (verses 18-19 of chapter 21).

Now, I just have to jump in here and say, wait a minute. We know many of the Apostles were killed and so were many of their followers, so we have some very odd verbiage here. What did Jesus mean when he said, "not a hair of your head will perish"? Perhaps he meant they would not lose their soul, but if this is so, then why would he use the phrase "hair of your head?" Souls are usually thought of as our true eternal identity, without the body. So, if we are doing a fresh and simple read here, no matter how uncomfortable this information seems, we should probably stick to what Jesus said, and just the way he said it. One thing we can think about, without manipulating the text, is the time frame of this prophecy. Remember that Jesus said the Good News would be preached in the whole world, and then the end would come (Matthew 24:14)? And, also remember that this "end" was not an ending of time, but tasks and/or events. So what was the task given to the disciples? It was basically to go out into the world, preach the Good News, and make disciples. So, it is right to say, within the context of this passage, that though the disciples are arrested, brought to trial, and even imprisoned, God would ensure their life until their task of spreading the Good News was completed. Also note that Matthew (24:14) writes, "…

this gospel of the kingdom will be preached in the whole world …" Do you see this slight variation in common thought? The idea here seems to be that the Good News is not preached to every living creature. Thus it is not preached "to" the whole world. It is as the phrasing says, preached "in" the whole world. As an example, if I preach the Good News of Jesus in one location in Kenya (today), it can be rightfully said that the Gospel has been preached in Kenya. We also know how the Good News spreads and what God's Spirit did to help the church grow in those early days. So, even if one small group of people became disciples in a whole country, that seed would spread out and eventually reach the whole region. Jesus knew this and foresaw it. The disciples also knew this. They realized that they did not need to reach every man, woman, boy, and girl in every region, by themselves. As far as their tasking from Jesus went, they just needed to plant the seeds in each region. Even after the disciples' death, that seed would spread over the whole earth. Looking at this whole situation, it is important to see that within their lifetime, the disciples did get the Good News of Jesus into every region of the known civilized world. They stayed true and faithful to the end of their task and the end of their lives.

Help I Am Surrounded

In the next section of Luke 21, we see the foretelling of Jerusalem being surrounded by its enemy. Let's look at this.

Luke 21:20-24

20 "When you see Jerusalem being surrounded by armies, you will know that its

**desolation is near. 21 Then let those who are
in Judea flee to the mountains, let those in the
city get out, and let those in the country not
enter the city. 22 For this is the time of
punishment in fulfillment of all that has been
written. 23 How dreadful it will be in those
days for pregnant women and nursing
mothers! There will be great distress in the
land and wrath against this people. 24 They
will fall by the sword and will be taken as
prisoners to all the nations. Jerusalem will
be trampled on by the Gentiles until the times
of the Gentiles are fulfilled.**

Proceed, if you will, to read this section freshly. What stands out and what is a mystery? Like the other two Gospels, there is an aspect of war and enemies of the Jews, but here Luke writes about surrounding armies and that when the disciples see the siege begin they will know that its desolation is near. If we marry this with the other two Gospels, it sounds like the prelude to the abomination that causes desolation is these armies surrounding Jerusalem. If this is accurate, then we can also say that the temple would be desecrated not long after the city is put under siege. This reasoning, however, is built on what we can see in scriptures, and the information is not very detailed. Thus, we are building this case on what seems like good logic and deduction. This means there is room for error, so we need to be careful here, right? Yes.

The next part of this passage mirrors the other two Gospel books. The disciples are told that when they see these things, they are to flee to the mountains. Luke adds that those out in the country, should not go back into the city. They need to go straight to the mountains. In the words of board-game slang: Don't pass Go and don't collect 200 dollars.

Now in verse 22, we get to some gritty stuff. Here Luke records Jesus as having said this time was a punishment that fulfills several prophecies – and these were prophecies that had already been written. Can you see this? At Jesus' time, he said "… in fulfillment of all that has been written." So, what Jesus was talking about was already written (no new writings). These would be the writings of the Old Testament that were over 400 years old. So, God had already planned to punish who? Well, I don't think it is a far stretch to see this: If Jesus said armies were going to surround Jerusalem and said his disciples needed to flee from there, something bad was going to happen to Jerusalem. So, I think we can rightfully say the punishment was going to be on Jerusalem (and possibly the whole nation). This was ordained before Jesus was even born. We don't hear this taught much – maybe because it is an uncomfortable idea. But this is what it seems that Luke is writing here (at least to me).

By the time we get down to verse 23, we see the same language that Matthew and Mark use. This time will be horrible for pregnant women and nursing mothers. In verses 23-24, those "in the land" will fall by the sword and be taken away as prisoners. This is pretty clear to me. It is a typical war of that era and it is brutal. Captives are often taken away to be slaves, far away from their home-land, so they cannot group together and fight against their oppressors. When they are in a strange land, they also have no homeland to fight for, so it pulls the teeth on large ambitious rebellions.

Late in verse 24, we come to an extremely important part of end-time prophecies. This one sentence is used and misused over and over to prove doctrines and theories. "Jerusalem will be trampled on by the Gentiles until the times of the Gentiles are fulfilled." Now, what does this mean? Well, my friend, this is where you need to do some serious homework. You need to search in Bible text and see where this type of phrasing is used. I promise you, there is similar imagery and phrasing in other prophetic places. Be careful, though. Try not to go to outside sources to figure this out. Many eschatologists try to assign 7 years of trouble here. This is hard to support, especially since history tells us that the war and siege of Jerusalem only lasted about 3 ½ years. In your research, you can start at Revelation 11:1-3. This is from verse 3:

> **"… it has been given to the Gentiles. They
> will trample on the holy city for 42 months."**

There Will Be Signs

We can look down a little further now. So, let's go to the 25th verse.

Luke 21:25-28

> **25 "There will be signs in the sun, moon and
> stars. On the earth, nations will be in
> anguish and perplexity at the roaring and
> tossing of the sea. 26 People will faint from
> terror, apprehensive of what is coming on the
> world, for the heavenly bodies will be shaken.
> 27 At that time they will see the Son of Man**

**coming in a cloud with power and great
glory. 28 When these things begin to take
place, stand up and lift up your heads,
because your redemption is drawing near."**

Do a Fresh Read, now. I know we have already read two other versions of this, so it will be really easy for your brain to "run home to mama." What I mean, is, when we see or hear things of a very familiar nature, our natural tendency is to file the information in the same slot as we did the last time. This mental filing system often shoves information away so fast that details are missed. So, again, let's see if we can notice any differences in Luke's account.

My take on this passage is that it includes the familiar sun, moon, and stars, but it just says that there will be signs in them. Luke does not record Jesus as having said that these heavenly bodies would stop shining or that any of them would fall. After the heavenly bodies are addressed, Luke says that Jesus begins talking about the earth. He says, "… nations will be in anguish and perplexed at the roaring and tossing of the sea."

There should be a very loud buzzer going off in your head about now because you need to use those RID rules. What in the world is Jesus talking about? It makes no common sense. There were storms on the Mediterranean Sea all the time and they were fierce, but no nation or group of people that I know of were in anguish over it, unless they lost loved ones or friends on the sea. Certainly, whole nations would not be upset because the sea was tossing and roaring. Even the larger local lakes, like the Sea of Galilee, could get pretty choppy at times, but no nation was ever upset about it. So, there must be something else going on. Since the beginning of the paragraph (according to NIV), is where the sun, moon, and stars are mentioned, we rightfully expect that the term "sea" is also a symbol that represents something else. So, "if it sounds weird, look it up" is the order of the day. Go over to your digital search tools and start looking up the term sea to see if there is any mention of this as a symbol, elsewhere in the Bible.

What did you find? I see these verses that might be helpful:

> **Isaiah 57:20 --- "But the wicked are like the tossing of the sea, which cannot rest, whose waves cast up mire and mud."**

> **Jude 1:12-13 --- "These people are blemishes at your love feasts, eating with you without the slightest qualm – shepherds who feed only themselves. They are clouds without rain, blown along by the wind, autumn trees, without fruit and uprooted – twice dead. They are wild waves of the sea, foaming up their shame, wandering stars, for whom blackest darkness has been reserved forever."**

There are some similar terms and ideas in these two passages, right? Is there a simple and direct connection between these verses and Luke 21? Hmm. Well, the Book of Jude may have been written after the book of Luke, so we might not be able to use it for previous prophetic references. This does not mean the symbolism cannot be used, however. There does seem to be a common theme here, at least in my view. Isaiah casts the wicked in a simile that calls for a parallel between the wicked and the tossing of the sea. This may be a comparison of how the sea's never-ending waves are similar to the wicked never stopping their wicked ways. In the Book of Jude, we see a similar comparison. The bad people at their love feasts are described as "… wild waves of the sea, foaming up their shame …" Both of these passages carry the image of what waves bring up. They are dredging up mud (maybe sin) and foaming up shame.

If we take the meaning of the simile in the two verses from Isaiah and Jude, we can deduce that what Jesus is saying is this:

> **The people in a nation that is full of wickedness are terrified about what is going on around them. They are in terrible apprehension about their future.**

Now, this is only one view and based on only three texts, so though this may very well be true, you will need to dig further and cross-check some things before you go and start teaching any of this. This is all part of a first, fresh and simple approach. It is best, but not foolproof. So, do your homework. ☺

One other thing that puts the wicked sea of people into a tizzy is that the heavenly bodies are shaken. Since we looked these up before we know that these likely represent the leaders of families, tribes, or a nation. Since we identified Jerusalem as the target of God's punishment, we can rightly say that the sea of wicked people is very afraid, like those in Jerusalem and the Judea area.

When this is all in place and happening, then Jesus steps in (verse 27), and comes in judgment (in clouds). When the disciples see all this coming down, then they are to pay attention (life up their heads), and watch intently, because they will shortly need to flee to the mountains (redemption), right?

So let me say here, that as you look at this passage of scripture, do you see any talk of the redeeming of men's souls? Why do you think it seems to be absent? Perhaps, because Jesus will have already paid for people's sins by the time this judgment comes – and the disciples will have already gone out and spread the Good News in every region. You be the judge. One thing seems pretty clear, though: This "redemption" that is drawing near is not the saving of souls. This is not the saving of the disciples' souls. That was already done. The disciples are saved, sanctified, filled with the Holy Spirit, and on the glory train to an eternal home with Jesus. The redemption here is about them leaving Jerusalem, physically, and thus being redeemed from the nation that turned their back on God. They were saved from the death and judgment that came on their fellow countrymen. At least this is my take, using a Fresh Read, with R.I.D rules.

The Inserted Parable

When we get down to Luke 21:29, we start reading a parable that Jesus inserted into his prophecy.

> **29 He told them this parable: "Look at the fig tree and all the trees. 30 When they sprout leaves, you can see for yourselves and know that summer is near. 31 Even so, when you**

**see these things happening, you know that
the kingdom of God is near. 32 "Truly I tell
you, this generation will certainly not pass
away until all these things have happened. 33
Heaven and earth will pass away, but my
words will never pass away.**

So, what do you think this parable is saying? It seems to be the same parable as in Matthew 24:32, though the wording is a little different. My question to you is this: Is the lesson clear here? Is it easy for a first-time reader to see a parallel between the ability of a person to tell what season is coming? If there is a cold wind coming down off the hills and birds seem to be gathering together in flocks, could autumn be coming soon? If you are in the winter season, and you see buds coming out on the trees or the first sprouting of leaves, could this be a sign that spring is coming very soon?   I think Jesus is expecting his disciples to have some common sense and see that this is not rocket science. Knowing all these terrible things were coming, likely put a lot of fear in the disciples. I am pretty sure that most people in this position would start to panic. In fact, as time went on, the believers could easily adopt a doomsday lifestyle and live in panic, as some Christian do today. In that panic state, everything that happened around them could be interpreted as a sign that the troubled times were starting. Jesus may have been trying to calm them down. I think, when I read this, Jesus is saying, hey guys, when all this stuff is about to happen, it will obvious – so don't panic. Now, you might read all this a little differently, but I think the content and intent of the parable are pretty clear.

For verses 32 and 33, the text is the same as in Matthew and Mark. Here again, the writer says clearly that the things Jesus is foretelling will happen within the generation of the disciples. None of the things Jesus foretold here seem to be for a thousand years or more in the future. How could Jesus say his disciples could easily see the signs and then flee Jerusalem, if the events were supposed to take place 2000 years later? If we take the text together and read it straight, it seems this troubled time was meant for the first century of the church. You may read all these texts differently and that is part of good Bible study. Not everyone is going to see things the same way.

The Final Passage

The last prophetic passage we are looking at in our Gospel books comparison starts in Luke 21:34. Let's go there.

> **34 "Be careful, or your hearts will be weighed down with carousing, drunkenness and the anxieties of life, and that day will close on you suddenly like a trap. 35 For it will come on all those who live on the face of the whole earth. 36 Be always on the watch, and pray that you may be able to escape all that is about to happen, and that you may be able to stand before the Son of Man."**

What are your first thoughts about this text? I see Jesus consoling his disciples again, and yet he is also warning them. As I was saying in previous comments, the disciples could easily become discouraged with the knowledge Jesus is giving them. They could panic and sort of go crazy. Now, what do many people do when they face unresolved trouble in their lives? They drink! And what do people do when they start thinking their lives or their lifestyles will end soon? They party! It is true. A common human answer to horrors is to exit normal life and go out in a flame of self-indulgence. The ideology is to get the most out of the tiny bit of life you have left; do all the things you feel you have been missing, or that so many around you are doing. Even Jesus' disciples were just human and they were constantly faced with temptations. They did sin and sometimes just fail in their attempts to be followers of Christ. These disciples he was talking to were also the ones who pledged loyalty and yet when they saw the danger, they all ran away, leaving Jesus alone to face his accusers. In the hour when he needed their support more than any other time, they abandoned him. Thus, Jesus knew what his disciples were made of. He knew how frail they were. His advice and warnings were exactly what they needed at that time and these words, too, were not lost on his disciples. They did remember his instructions and it helped them through those very bad times.

Chapter 8

What Have We Gained?

Here's a little riddle for you: There were ten cats on top of a car and one jumped off. How many were left? We would all likely say nine, right? Well, the official answer is, none. Do you know why? Because they were all copy cats!

When it comes to teaching prophecy, there are well over a million copy cats on planet earth. It seems that Bible teachers both great and small, mostly repeat what they have been taught or whatever literature is sent to them by scholars that think the same way. Unfortunately, very few Bible teachers seem to take the time to search scripture to see how it stands on its own - that is, without reading between the lines or filling in information that is not clearly presented. Here's where we error as true scholars of God's Word. If we go into scripture with preconceived ideas and read every text with premade filters in our heads, we can make the Bible mean anything we want. For instance, there is a whole group of scholars who view the Bible as a guide to spiritual principles. This group believes that nothing in the Bible should be taken literally and that it was all penned as a collection of spiritual lessons. If this were true, it would make God's Word just another book of philosophy, rather than an account of what God has done and is doing for mankind. As I have said, please read prophetic texts with open eyes and with a desire for truth. If you take an honest and fresh approach each time you read it, you will more likely gain a better understanding of what the text says, rather than someone's conjectures.

Some Pre-Thoughts

We have spent a lot of time looking at Jesus' prophetic words and comparing the different versions. Personally, I find this all both fascinating and tedious. By nature, I am not a very patient person, so I tend to gravitate toward short tasks that I can complete in less than an hour. Thus, this whole study, so far, has truly been a mountain. However, the climb seems to have been worthwhile, and there was no other way to get the nitty-gritty of what Jesus said, and what he didn't say. If you have a firm grasp of what we discussed and did your homework, you should already be pretty well equipped to discuss eschatology with other scholars. Oh, excuse me, did I say, "discuss"? The unfortunate reality of this situation is that with the knowledge you have, you will more like have heated debates. Why? I am not sure, but it seems there is no hotter topic, nor one that is more closely guarded than end-time doctrine. It seems to be everyone's private golden egg that no-one is allowed to touch. Scholars seem to be able to discuss several other important Christian doctrines without flared nostrils, but enter the holy land of end-times and the boxing gloves come off. Yikes! In all honesty, in the last 20 years or more I have heard less debate and seen fewer frothy mouths over the divinity of Christ than over when he was (or is) to return. How did we as Christians ever come to this place? Have we put our traditions and imaginations above God's Word? Have we as the church of Christ, decided to fill in information between the written lines of the Bible? Have we decided to make the Bible what we want it to be? When what we read becomes uncomfortable, do we claim that it doesn't say what it clearly does? Do we run away from its morals or its direction for living a Godly life?

Now, there are a lot of questions here, and we are certainly not going to answer them in this book. But if we are more purists when it comes to God's Word, and if we want to protect the meaning of the original manuscripts, then these questions deserve an answer. Interestingly enough, many of these questions can be answered by the Bible itself, if we let it. So, I encourage you to keep reading and keep digging. Know what the Word says and stick to it. Reinforce it in your mind and heart. Keep up the text purification process. What do I mean? I mean keep going back to the Word again and again with a cleared head and no agenda. Keep asking yourself this: What does this text actually say, without any outside help?

The Gain – or Not

The big question at this point is whether we truly gained anything by comparing the three Gospel book accounts. I think we can agree that going over Jesus' words with a magnifying glass has some real value, especially when we are trying to weed out the false ideas that are often thrown into them. So, there is some obvious gain in knowing what Jesus said. However, after going through a fairly detailed comparison, was there additional insight about end-times? Hmm. I could be doubtful. After all, the accounts are quite similar. But, before we count the time we spent as trash, let's briefly look at some larger factors we have not yet talked about.

History of the Books

This is what the website "bible.org" says (sorry, you cannot click on this as a link - ☺)

> **The Gospels are dated traditionally as follows: Mark is believed to be the first gospel written around A.D. 60. Matthew and Luke follow and are written between A.D. 60-70; John is the final gospel, written between A.D. 90-100. The internal evidence supports these early dates for several reasons.**

Now honestly, we cannot take any of these dates as fact. These are educated estimates, combined with tradition. For Instance, the writing date for the Book of John is highly controversial and often disputed. However, if we take what we have as information, we may see some reasons for what we found in our comparisons. If Mark wrote his account first, then his text (or parts of it) may have been available for reference when Matthew and Luke wrote their accounts. If Mark's writings were considered reliable and if they had been tested for accuracy, then it would have seemed right for Matthew and Luke to build on what Mark provided. Perhaps more facts and testimonies emerged after Mark's writings, and Mathew and Luke wanted to add those things into their writings. It is also possible that Matthew or Luke wanted to portray a different view of Christ and his life. One writer, for instance, may want to focus more on Jesus as the Son of God, whereas another writer might want to show that though Jesus was divine, he often showed his character as a common man. Still another writer might not want to emphasize any particular aspect, and write more with the idea of "just the facts, ma'am." If you read an analysis of the four Gospel books, you will see comments about this very thing. One writer did seem to lean toward one aspect and another writer leaned another way. I don't want to be the spoiler of that surprise, so I will let you research this on your own. It is easy to find on the internet and when you look this up, you will also find other interesting aspects about the writers of the Gospels. By the way, if you have not yet heard the term, "synoptic" Gospels in the Bible, you might want to look into this.

Were the Differences Significant?

Since the comparison of the Gospel books was so lengthy, I think it would be good to briefly review some of the more important differences. So, if you don't mind, I will try to compile the information in an easier way to see it. If you don't want or need this review, then you can just skip this chapter and move on to the next subject.

Matthew to Mark Comparison Outline

Mark 13:1-4

Mark recorded the disciples' inquiry as "Tell us … what will be the sign that they are to be fulfilled," whereas Matthew recorded "Tell us … what will be the sign of your coming and of the end of the age?" There may not be a significant difference between the writer's intentions, but when avid eschatologists get ahold of these verses, they can become walls of contention. For instance, if I just said these things in today's language, with common meaning, it might sound something like this:

1. Mark: What is it that indicates when the things you talked about are going to happen?

2. Matthew: What is it that indicates when you will return and when the current age ends?

<u>Mark 13: 5-8</u>

The high points in this section include a former point about how Jesus' statement "the end is still to come," refers to the ending of tasks or events, not the end of a time-period. There is foretelling of wars and nations at war, which came to pass in the first century of the church - and there is a prophecy about earthquakes and famines, which seemed to naturally accompany the wars.

<u>Mark 13:9-13</u>

Mark focuses on a different aspect than Matthew in that Matthew wrote "persecuted and put to death," whereas Mark wrote, "flogged." Mark also, at this point, anyway, does not talk about how people will turn away from the faith. It seems to me that Mark emphasizes the spreading of the Good News, more than other things. Mark does include the aspect and role of the Holy Spirit in this whole future scenario. He records Jesus as having said that when the disciples are brought before leaders/rulers, the Holy Spirit will give them what they are to say. Mark indicates that Jesus said it would be the Holy Spirit speaking, not them.

Mark 13:14-19

What did Jesus say for the disciples to watch for? The "abomination that causes desolation," as described in the Book of Daniel. This is the desecration of the temple. Mark also emphases this key Old Testament prophecy that Jesus talks about. This one aspect seems to stick out like a skin sore. It tends to be a hinge for all that followed. Here Jesus is telling his followers to watch for the sign and when they see it, flee town and go far away to the mountains.

Mark 13:21-27

Jesus warns of false Messiahs and prophets that will appear after he ascends. Of course, even as it is today, someone is always trying to capitalize on someone else's fame. In the perceived vacuum of power after Christ's crucifixion, there were bound to be opportunists who would try to "pick up" where Jesus left off. Of course, Jesus' foretelling came to pass in vivid color. Many did rise and tried to establish a following that was patterned after Jesus' success. Sadly, a lot of people followed these false leaders. Some of them had an agenda of raising an army to fight against the Romans, but none succeeded. One aspect we did not discuss when we looked at Matthew 24, is that these heavenly bodies (sun, moon, and stars) are part of Old Testament passages from the prophet

Isaiah (13:9-10 and 34:1-4). One important thing in framing the parameters of Jesus' words in Mark 13 (and Matthew 24) is seeing that the words in Isaiah were a foretelling of judgments that happened before Jesus. This is crucial in good eschatology. If the sun was darkened, the moon did not give its light, and the stars fell from the sky, when God carried these judgments out against ancient Babylon and other ancient nations, and yet, the world did not burn up or end, then we cannot conclude that Jesus was prophesying the end of the world. Regardless of what these symbolic phrases mean to us today, Jesus was not foretelling the end of mankind, the doom of the planet, or anything close to that.

<u>Mark 13:32-37</u>

The one thing that seems to be missing here is the part where Matthew records Jesus as having talked about this era of time being like the days of Noah. The whole comparison is missing in Mark. Also, the talk of two people being in a place; one taken and the other left, is not included in Mark. Instead of the Noah-days discourse, Mark goes on talking about the responsibility of the servants to keep doing their assigned tasks, faithfully. This corresponds more with the 45th verse in Matthew 24.

The final warning/instruction here in Mark is clear and precise: "Watch!" So, let's review this one more time, because as we said that it seems to be a major pivot for events. What were the disciples watching for? Jesus to swoop down and take them up to Heaven? Is this what the text in Matthew or Mark actually says? Are the disciples to watch for earthquakes, floods, or famines? Are they to look for wars, the Mark of the Beast, the

Anti-Christ, global universal churches, or one world government? How about chips under people's skin?

Luke to Matthew and Mark

<u>Luke 21:1-11</u>

In Luke's account, Jesus' disciples were talking about the beauty of the temple because of its stones and the gifts that people had brought to the temple. It seems to me that this is a little more detailed that the other accounts. Matthew and Mark wrote in a little more general terms, whereas Luke is more specific about what the disciples find beautiful about the temple.

It seems that Luke doesn't use the term "false prophet," He more generically says that many men will claim they are the real Jesus. These could have tried to present themselves as the resurrected Jesus since the disciples and many others had seen and reported that Jesus was alive after his crucifixion. Other imposters may have presented themselves as the returned Jesus since Jesus had prophesied that he would return. Luke writes similarly to Matthew and Mark, here. There is mention of wars and what the NIV translates as "uprisings." This is interesting to me because there was a major uprising by the Zealots in the Jerusalem/Judea area that caused the Romans to come in and eventually lay siege to Jerusalem, and place rigid restrictions on the surrounding area.

When we get down to verse 11, we again see the foretelling of earthquakes and famines, but Luke adds pestilence, as well as fearful events and great signs from heaven. There could be some significance here, so it would be prudent to search in the Old Testament for other prophecies of pestilence and see if they are connected with war and/or God's judgment.

One difference I can see in chapter 21, is that Luke does not talk about the sun, moon, or stars in the same way that the other two Gospel books do. Early in the chapter, he makes more of a general statement about there will be "fearful events and great signs from heaven."   Since Luke writes about Jesus saying these things in about the same order or placement as where the sun, moon, and stars statement appears in the other two Gospel books, we are probably fairly safe in thinking that Luke is writing about the same events as Matthew and Mark, just being more general. To be fair, Luke does mention the sun, moon, and stars, later, in verse 25, but this is not in the sequence that it appears in the other two books.

<u>Luke 21:12-19</u>

Some wording in this passage is similar to Matthew 24 and Mark 13, but the events are not told in the same order. In Matthew 24:9, for instance, the wording is "then," indicating what comes next. Here in Luke, it seems that the same or similar events are said to be before what was said in the previous verses. Why is this important? Because a pure and fresh study never takes things out of context – which also means, it cannot be taken out of the time-context that is specifically given in scripture.

One important thing I noticed in this passage is where Jesus said, the words and the wisdom that the Holy Spirit was going to give, were going to be irresistible, even for their enemies. At this, I just have to say, wow. No man can do this.

In verse 18, there is an interesting change in verbiage, when compared to the other two Gospels. Both Matthew and Mark use the phrase "but the one who stands firm to the end will be saved" (13th verse), but Luke writes "But not a hair of your head will perish. Stand firm, and you will win life (verses 18-19 of chapter 21).

Luke 21:20-24

Like the other two Gospels, there is an aspect of war and enemies of the Jews, but here Luke writes about surrounding armies and that when the disciples see the siege begin they will know that its desolation is near. The disciples are told that when they see these things, they are to flee to the mountains. Luke adds that those who are out in the country should not go back into the city. Now in verse 22, Matthew records Jesus as having said this what would happen in this time period was a punishment that fulfills several prophecies – and these are prophesies that had been written hundreds of years before Jesus' time.

Late in verse 24, we come to an extremely important part of end-time prophecies: "Jerusalem will be trampled on by the Gentiles until the times of the Gentiles are fulfilled." Now, what does this mean? Many eschatologists try to assign 7 years of trouble here. This is hard to support, especially since history tells us that the war and siege of Jerusalem only lasted about 3 ½ years. For research, you can start at Revelation 11:1-3. This is from verse 3:

> **"… it has been given to the Gentiles. They will trample on the holy city for 42 months."**

<u>Luke 21:25-28</u>

This passage includes the familiar sun, moon, and stars, but it just says that there will be signs in them. Luke does not record Jesus as having said that these heavenly bodies would stop shining or that any of them would fall. After the heavenly bodies are addressed, Jesus begins talking about the earth. He says, "… nations will be in anguish and perplexed at the roaring and tossing of the sea." What in the world is Jesus talking about? These verses may help:

> **Isaiah 57:20 --- "But the wicked are like the tossing of the sea, which cannot rest, whose waves cast up mire and mud."**

> **Jude 1:12-13 --- "These people are blemishes at your love feasts, eating with you without the slightest qualm – shepherds who feed only themselves. They are clouds without rain, blown along by the wind, autumn trees, without fruit and uprooted – twice dead. They are wild waves of the sea, foaming up their shame, wandering stars, for whom blackest darkness has been reserved forever."**

One other thing that puts the wicked sea of people into a tizzy is that the heavenly bodies are shaken. Since we looked these up before we know that these likely represent the leaders of families, tribes, or a nation. Since we identified Jerusalem as the target of God's punishment, we can rightly say that the sea of wicked people, that are very afraid, are like those in Jerusalem and the Judea area.

Summary

As you can see from the outline above, there are some interesting differences between the Gospel books' versions of Jesus' prophetic words. Are there any doctrinal differences? No. These accounts are very homogenous. We may gain some additional information in one account, versus another – and we may more clearly see what the authors are saying, by hearing the prophecies in slightly different wording. I find it helpful.

Let me encourage you in this way: If you end up teaching a class on end-times, try to include the prophetic writings of all three synoptic Gospels books. This will help round out the end-times views and assist in removing views that are based on picky semantics.

Chapter 9

When Does the Kingdom Come?

If you have children or have ever been in a car with children, you have probably heard the question, "Are we there yet?" Well, if you were not there yet, and were still a long way from being "there," the question was likely to emerge again and again. At that point, you likely found the queries quite tiresome and even annoying.

I think when we study end-times, the whole process can also become tiresome and sometimes right down annoying. Many Christians I have talked to don't even want to study end-times doctrine. Why do you suppose this is? Well, I think, for one thing, it has been taught, preached seminar-ed, and movie-d, to death! I hear radio and television preachers that dedicate about a whole month out of every year, to teaching about end-time prophecies - then through the rest of the year, they will make mention of it in other sermons. Why do you suppose this is? Well, first, think about this: Of all the topics the Bible teaches, if we give proper and balanced teaching of all the doctrines of the Bible, we probably won't be circling back to end-times for a matter of years, not months. So, again, why do many preachers talk about end-time prophecies, so much? Do you know what I think? I think the bottom line is that doomsday theories sell. I suppose it might seem a bit crass to say this, but I am going to be bold here and say, in strictly a business sense, the church may use doomsday teaching in the same way Hollywood uses sex and violence. Some ministers use it because it sells. It sells air time, books, and videos. There is also a perception that doomsday sells salvation. That is, people get saved as a result of telling them that disaster is just around the corner, but that if you follow the preacher's instructions you can be saved from all of it. But is this even what the Bible teaches? Maybe; maybe not. It is your job as a Christian and a scholar to look into God's Word and weed out doctrines that do not stand up to sensible scrutiny – then hold on firmly to the unshakable things.

The Kingdom

Especially in the Bible's Gospel books, there is a fair amount of talk about "the kingdom." Sometimes the word "kingdom" is by itself and at other times it is used with heaven or God – so, "Kingdom of Heaven," or "Kingdom of God." When we see prophetic statements that include these phrases, we can be at a loss about their meaning, and we never want to be in the dark about scripture unless God has purposely veiled information for our protection (see my book "THE VEIL" – on Amazon and Kindle). So, I want to again visit what these phrases mean and then move on to talking about when this comes. If we cannot understand when and how this kingdom comes, then we are going to miss much of the meaning of prophecy.

Research

I know we have talked about this before, but as a reminder, I am going to cover this one more time:

Let's focus first on what we see in Matthew as "the kingdom of heaven?" In a simple phrase search, I found there are over 30 verses in the Bible that have the phrase "kingdom of heaven." However, this exact phrase does not appear in any other book of the Bible. So, it seems this phrase was only used by Matthew. Perhaps one mystery here is that Mark uses "kingdom of heaven" in many places, but in at least one other place, he uses the phrase "kingdom of God."

Before we explore other Biblical references, let's look at the term itself. In Greek, it seems a kingdom that is from or in the "heavens" is a celestial idea. To pagans, there were several gods in the heavens. Each one of them could have had a kingdom, or some may have shared the heavens as a ruling place or kingdom. So, perhaps the phrase, kingdom of heaven, is more generic, where "kingdom of God" is more specifically the heavenly kingdom that belongs to, or is ruled by, Jehovah God. Okay, back to our text study.

Possibly the biggest clue to what this phrase means comes from Matthew chapters 3, 4, 5, and 9. Here is where we learn that John the Baptist came preaching "Repent for the kingdom of heaven is near." After John was imprisoned, Jesus began to preach the same message, and when Jesus sent out his disciples, he told them to preach the message that "The kingdom of heaven is near." So part of the gospel message seemed to include this idea that people needed to straighten out their lives and live in a Godly manner because there was a heavenly kingdom that was near them.

When, Indeed

Now, there is something larger in this picture that is easily missed. When people read "The kingdom of heaven is near," they tend to hear "The kingdom of Heaven is coming soon." But, the Greek words don't say this. One clue is that the NIV version (and others) use the phrase, "Repent, for the kingdom of heaven has come near." John and Jesus, both used this phrasing. It was an action that included the recent past, now, and the future. It was something that was not a prophecy of just future events. Thus, we might say in today's English, "God's kingdom is here, now. It has arrived and it is going to stay." We also get some clues from Matthew 17:20-21

> **"Once, on being asked by the Pharisees when the kingdom of God would come, Jesus replied, "The coming of the kingdom of God is not something that can be observed, nor will people say, 'Here it is,' or 'There it is,' because the kingdom of God is in your midst."**

Here, it seems Jesus is even more clearly saying that the kingdom of God was there, right then and that it was among them.

Let me ask you a question: Who was representing the kingdom of God or the kingdom of Heaven on earth? The answer is obviously, Jesus. He is the one who is described as the "king of kings." When a king came into another country (in ancient times), and had his envoy with him, it could be said that the country the king represented had "come." So, in a real sense, John proclaimed (as the forerunner) that the King had already arrived, so make preparations for him (in your heart). Jesus continued to proclaim that he, the King, had arrived – but no one fully understood what either John or Jesus were saying. It was hidden from them.

So, what is the answer to this question "When did the Kingdom of God (or the kingdom of heaven) come? In light of the text we read, it appears it came to earth when Jesus arrived, or at least when Jesus began his ministry (when baptized).

How Can This Be?

How can the coming of the Kingdom of God or heaven be when Jesus arrived, when some prophetic statements seem to refer to a later coming?

To answer this quandary takes a lot of research. So, you need to dig into this to make some sense of it. I took a fairly good look into this while I am in the process of writing this, and here is what I found: It appears to me that the Kingdom of God or Heaven is not talked about in the Old Testament. This concept doesn't seem to be part of the Law or prophets. However, I think we can see some shadows of these things. We do know that the throne of David was to never end. It was foretold that the Messiah would come and sit on his throne and his kingdom would not end. Also, the text that Jesus used to stump the Jewish leaders was this: How could David say, The Lord says to my lord: "Sit at my right hand until I make your enemies a footstool for your feet?" David was declaring his offspring to be his Lord (Psalms 110). So, in all this, there is talk of an eternal kingdom, though it seems in prophecy it was more considered to be the seat of King David and ruling over the nation of Judah (and, possibly Israel). Perhaps, since the Jews rejected Christ (and Jesus knew they would), the term of this eternal throne changed. Perhaps this kingdom that Jesus said was going to be taken away from the Jews and given to those who would honor God, was then to be called the Kingdom of God, or heaven. Thus it did not belong to a specific race or nation on earth, instead, it belonged to those who belonged to God – the believers. These could be Jews by bloodline, or any other race of people who became believers in Christ.

So what about the New Testament? Are there prophecies that talk about the Kingdom coming later – after Jesus' ascension? Hmm. Well, oddly enough, I don't see any conclusive scriptures that absolutely place the coming of God's kingdom at a later date. I don't see any proof that God's kingdom comes to earth later, or that the thousand-year reign of Christ on earth, is the beginning of his reign or his kingdom on earth. The only scriptures that seem undeniable are the ones we discussed, where Jesus told his followers that the kingdom of heaven (or of God) was near them – and right in their midst.

And Then There are Parables - Again

If we look a little deeper, we can find many parable lessons where Jesus is talking about the Kingdom. These were mostly handled in the second chapter of this book. As an overview, we see text in these parables that seem to say people are thrown out of the kingdom, or not allowed to go in - and this ejection (or rejection) brings weeping and gnashing of teeth. The region outside the Kingdom also is described as outer darkness. So there is this obvious concept that from Jesus' time forward, there will be people in the Kingdom and people who are not.

One issue that is highly debated is when this separation occurs. Some scholars say at each person's death, some say this occurred when Jesus judged the Jewish nation in 70 AD, while others say there will be a final judgment at the end of time (end of the earth as we know it) and this final judgment will determine who will be in the Kingdom and who will not. This last idea seems to be missing some elements of doctrine in the Bible, however. What about people who died before the end of the world? Where do they go? Jesus said to the thief on the cross he would be with him in Paradise, that very day. But, Paul said he was taken up to Paradise when he had the visions of Heaven. So, there are several disparities in the beliefs of eschatology experts. How do we resolve these issues? By carefully examining each of the texts presented by those who argue a specific view. If we read each one straight, with no manipulation, and in context, we should easily see the time-frame of foretold events. If the text is symbolic, it may be harder to pin down the time-frame, but this is okay. If the time-frame is not specific, then let it be so. Conclude that Jesus did not want to reveal that time frame or the Father had not revealed it to him.

To do an extremely thorough review of the "Kingdom coming," you would need to read all of the parables in

Matthew, Mark, and Luke - go over them with a fine-tooth comb - and analyze each in a way that allows you to pull out text applicable to the Kingdom of God and when it is in operation.

Now, I went through many of these parables to just see how many places talk about the Kingdom, and my impression, again, was that there is no solid proof or direction in them. What I mean is that I could not nail down a time-frame that was consistent in all the parables. Some sounded like the Kingdom was in operation and had members right then, while other parables seemed to talk about actions by God for future events. Since there seems to be a mixture of time-frames, perhaps Jesus was portraying a concept that God was already in the weeding process and intended to keep that going to the future. Does this mean there is no future judgment of people? I would say, it is more likely there is a future judgment, but exactly how that is done, is open to debate. Again, because this is so controversial, you will need to explore this well to form your own educated opinion.

The Lord's Prayer

Before we look at Jesus' reference to God's kingdom in the Lord's Prayer, let me say that this prayer was clearly given as an example of how to make a simple prayer (unlike what the heathens were doing). Jesus was not trying to give a hard format that we had to adopt. In fact, there is nowhere in the Bible that records anyone using this prayer or anything close to it. Jesus was not recorded praying this prayer after he gave the example, and neither did any of his disciples, including Paul. If they did use this prayer, it is not historically documented.

There are other prayers throughout the New Testament, by Jesus, some of his original disciples, and by Paul, but none seem to be in this exact format and none of them parrot Jesus' original prayer words.

Now to the chase. Let's look at Matthew's version of the Lord's Prayer:

Matthew 6:9-13

> **"Our Father in heaven, hallowed be your name, 10 your kingdom come, your will be done, on earth as it is in heaven. 11 Give us today our daily bread. 12 And forgive us our debts,   as we also have forgiven our debtors. 13 And lead us not into temptation, but deliver us from the evil one."**

Notice the phrases "your kingdom come, your will be done, on earth as it is in heaven." This can be improperly phrased and misunderstood when taught or preached. It is easy to mentally skip over the part that says "your will be done." If we do this, then the prayer says, essentially, "your kingdom come on earth as it is in heaven." However, this is not a solid conclusion to this prayer. You need to look at the Greek manuscript. The punctuation marks are not used in the same way as here or in other translations. The interpreters have to put in the English punctuation to bring out the correct meaning from the ancient manuscript. When we look at this carefully, we see that the thought flow is not necessarily carried through. The first phrase is definitely, "your kingdom come," and the second phrasing seems to be "your will be done" - but was the writer trying to say that both should be on earth the way it is in heaven? Possibly so, but it may be debatable. Either way, the idea seems to be that God's will be done (which would include his kingdom on earth).

There is also a larger issue here and it goes to the same one that we have been dealing with in this chapter. We need to see if there are any indicators about when the Kingdom was to come. I think we answered this question with some satisfaction, yet a verse like, "… your kingdom come, your will be done, on earth as it is in heaven" (vs 10) can resurrect certain aspects of the original question. So, let's see if we can deal with what this verse is trying to say concerning time frames. The first thing we will need to deal with is our perspective when we read it. If I come into this verse assuming the Kingdom of God has not yet come, or not fully come, then I am going to read the verse this way: Lord, establish your Kingdom (in the near or far future), and your will, on the earth, in the same way that you have established it in heaven. However, if I listen to Jesus' words about the Good News (the kingdom of heaven is near – or among you), and assume the Kingdom of God is already on earth, then I am going to read this verse more this way: Father, I agree with you about establishing your Kingdom on earth, so may your will be done on earth, as it has been established in heaven.

Because we were able to make a fairly strong case from our previous exploration of the Word in regards to what the kingdom of heaven is, let's assume that Jesus is the King of this heavenly kingdom and that he is on earth as a representative of that kingdom. Our question must then be, "Who are the subjects of Jesus' heavenly kingdom? I would say, his subjects on earth are likely the disciples, to start. Later, it would be all who follow him and are loyal to him as their king, right? If this reasoning is sound (and you will need to judge whether it is, in light of scripture), then the more believers there are on planet earth, the larger Jesus' kingdom. Thus, the kingdom is increasingly established on earth. And, just as God had his kingdom, authority, and subjects in heaven, so, later he had the same on earth. It is pretty simple when you think about it. It is not rocket science. Still, all this needs to be cross-checked and purified by other passages that deal with this subject.

Maybe in the end it doesn't matter how we read or phrase verse 10. Whether Jesus is establishing his kingdom on earth, or whether just his coming is established, it is kind of superfluous. When Jesus arrived, it was an irreversible truth that God was establishing his kingdom on earth and that he would continue until his plan was complete. So, here is another brain teaser: When did God finish establishing his Kingdom? Hmm. Well, since God knows the future and can make it happen, in a real sense God's Kingdom was established at Jesus' time, yet until the last soul has been saved and granted eternal life, the Kingdom's establishment is not complete. At least this is the way scripture seems to present the kingdom of heaven. But, you do your own research and see how you divide the text.

Chapter 10

More Yeast. We Need to Rise

It takes time and effort to make good bread, so a bright engineer thought he would create a machine to do the job. Great idea, right? I guess you could say it was a successful venture because when they hit the market a lot of people bought the bread-making machines. Now, they were a little pricey for poor people, so many people who wanted them were not able to get them right away. After a few years, the excitement abated and sales dropped off. A few years later - I believe it was during the holiday season - some newer models that were less expensive were advertised. Enthusiasm for the machines surged, and future garage sale fodder started showing up under Christmas trees across America.

One of these machines also showed up in our household, and we all waited in anticipation for those baking-bread fragrances. Soon, the new bread-making machine was put into action, and careful attention was given to the printed instructions. The first loaf was wonderful, and as a result, our supply of butter became seriously depleted. Now, the loaves were not quite as large as the ones you buy in the store, but we were okay with that since it seemed quite easy to make the loaves. After all, you just put the stuff in, turn it on, and forget it, right? Life was grand because we had access to freshly baked bread - and even rolls! Now, I suppose the adage, "If it sounds too good to be true, it probably is," could be applied to many bread machines, because the great machine we hailed as our new joy, started to diminish in performance. The first few loaves were great and met all the specifications, but then without warning, the machine began producing smaller loaves. The bread was just not rising as much as it was supposed to. We thought it might be defective, but the manufacturer assured us it was right and that we just needed to put the ingredients in correctly. Others we talked to, who had the same problems, seemed to find solutions by using different yeast. Others said we needed to make sure we used cold water. We tried everything others had found helpful but were never able to reproduce full loaves again. As time went by, the machine that was not very cheap, sat on the shelf and was used less and less.

So, what was wrong with our new "toy?" Well, we don't know. Since I have a background in electronic and electric troubleshooting, I took a look at the machine and its functions on a couple of occasions. My best guestimate was that the machine was supposed to warm the bread mixture during its rising cycle, and it either stopped doing that or reduced the amount of heated time. Why or how I am not sure. I would guess it was a flaw in the design or the machines were fragile. The final solution was the purchase of a heavy-duty mixer that had bread paddles, so we could make bread a different way.

The bottom line? We didn't ever have fresh bread as often.
Thus ends my sad and real tale of fresh bread – or not.

Should There Be Rising?

Properly made bread rises, right? Yes, there is a flatbread that
has no yeast, but most people prefer nicely raised bread. It is
just fluffier. But, what if you add yeast to bread and do all the
right things, yet it still does not rise? You are disappointed,
right? This is true for other things in life also. If we take the
right steps, we have expectations that certain things are going
to happen. When things don't go as expected, then we are
disappointed. Sometimes, we can even become angry.

God makes plans, also. His plans allow for everything to go
right, and for everything to go wrong - but our reality is
somewhere between. Some things go perfectly and some do
not. Why? Well, partly because this is God's specific will and
partly because he uses time and chance to affect our lives.

Ecclesiastes 9:11

> **"I have seen something else under the sun:**
> **The race is not to the swift or the battle to the**
> **strong, nor does food come to the wise or**
> **wealth to the brilliant or favor to the learned;**
> **but time and chance happen to them all."**

Okay, let's admit here that we don't hear many sermons based
on this scripture. It is uncomfortable and goes against the grain
of our American ideology to think that God allows time and

chance to affect our lives. However, this dovetails into what Paul wrote.

Romans 8:28

> **"And we know that all things work together
> for good to them that love God, to them who
> are the called according to his purpose."**

If we consider the basic idea Paul is writing about here, we need to consider that under "all things" are events that God did not specifically manipulate into being. If what happens "naturally" serves God's purpose – or can be made to serve God's purpose, then why would an almighty God, waste time and energy creating something that gives the same result? We know that God is very wise, and even a very wise human being can see the wisdom of God's choice in this matter.

So, we can say that even random events can and are used by God. When we apply these principles to death and resurrection, we can relax a little and know that the process is part of God's plans. They are set in motion and cannot be escaped. The bottom line may be that the "when and how" are superfluous questions and don't need to be answered at all. After all, God does not answer to us, we answer to him. He does not have to tell us about death and resurrection at all. He does seem to give us glimpses into these things and sometimes these can offer us some comfort because we can then see he has it all under control.

When the Resurrection Begins.

Though the question of when the resurrection occurs may not be all that important if we are responsible scholars we need to make sure we know the landscape of Biblical discussions. As good apologists, we need to have good answers to questions about our faith. So, let's dive into this study, using our R.I.D rules.

Right up front, we need to know that there are many views of resurrection and its timing. One view is that there is "soul sleep." This view can be described in the following manner:

> **"Soul sleep" is the belief that the souls of Christians who die will "rest" in an inert state until Christ's future return. Soul sleep is sometimes referred to as Christian mortalism or psychopannychism. Regardless of the terms, it is a belief that the souls of believers do not immediately go to be with Christ upon the death of the body. Ecclesiastes 9:5, 12:7, and Psalms 115:17 are used to support this doctrine.**

One classic view of resurrection is that the soul goes to be with Christ in heaven (or Paradise) when the body dies. What Jesus said to the thief on the cross (Luke 23:43) is one of many texts used to support this doctrine.

Other doctrines include a divided resurrection, where some go to heaven at one time, then others come later.

After considering all these views, we can see that we have a lot of work to do to sort out the truth. As we look through some scriptures, we need to be especially mindful of what the specific writer was trying to convey. We need to set aside our personal beliefs and put aside any agenda we have of trying to prove anything. Only when we lay down all of our agendas, will we be able to truly read the text anew and glean the real meaning of the text, as it was written.

Text to Consider

Here are some of the texts we need to consider when we are sorting out this business of resurrection.

John 5:25-29

> **"Truly, truly, I say to you, an hour is coming and now is, when the dead will hear the voice of the Son of God, and those who hear will live."**

John 6:39

> **"This is the will of Him who sent me, that of all that He has given me I lose nothing, but raise it up on the last day."**

John 6:54

> **"He who eats my flesh and drinks my blood has eternal life, and I will raise him up on the last day."**

Now, in all fairness, I encourage you to read all the text before and after these verses, before you proceed with this study. You may even want to look at different translations, so you get the "lay of the land."

Let's dive into this now and look first at John 5:25-29. What John wrote about what Jesus said, sounds like this to me: I am telling you the absolute truth about this.

> **There will be a time, which has already**
> **started, when the dead will hear Jesus' voice**
> **and will live, because of it.**

Now, as you read this passage, you may see it differently – and this is okay.

I think we can agree that Jesus is being emphatic about what he wants the disciples to hear. The big question is what exactly was Jesus saying to his disciples? I think there is no way to vet this without looking at the whole speech, so let's go back to the 16th verse and read on.

John 5:16-30

> **16 So, because Jesus was doing these things**
> **on the Sabbath, the Jewish leaders began to**
> **persecute him. 17 In his defense Jesus said to**
> **them, "My Father is always at his work to**
> **this very day, and I too am working." 18 For**
> **this reason they tried all the more to kill him;**
> **not only was he breaking the Sabbath, but he**
> **was even calling God his own Father, making**
> **himself equal with God.**

> **9 Jesus gave them this answer: "Very truly I**
> **tell you, the Son can do nothing by himself;**
> **he can do only what he sees his Father doing,**
> **because whatever the Father does the Son**

also does. 20 For the Father loves the Son and shows him all he does. Yes, and he will show him even greater works than these, so that you will be amazed. 21 For just as the Father raises the dead and gives them life, even so the Son gives life to whom he is pleased to give it. 22 Moreover, the Father judges no one, but has entrusted all judgment to the Son, 23 that all may honor the Son just as they honor the Father. Whoever does not honor the Son does not honor the Father, who sent him. 24 "Very truly I tell you, whoever hears my word and believes him who sent me has eternal life and will not be judged but has crossed over from death to life. 25 Very truly I tell you, a time is coming and has now come when the dead will hear the voice of the Son of God and those who hear will live. 26 For as the Father has life in himself, so he has granted the Son also to have life in himself. 27 And he has given him authority to judge because he is the Son of Man. 28 "Do not be amazed at this, for a time is coming when all who are in their graves will hear his voice 29 and come out— those who have done what is good will rise to live, and those who have done what is evil will rise to be condemned. 30 By myself I can do nothing; I judge only as I hear, and my judgment is just, for I seek not to please myself but him who sent me.

After a Fresh Read of this whole passage, we should be getting a better picture of the subject matter surrounding Jesus' statements about resurrection.

The first thing to note is that Jesus was technically breaking Mosaic Law by healing people on the Sabbath. It was considered "work," and thus not allowed. Jesus told them that his Father (God) was always at work. In other words, Jesus was saying that God was his Father and he did not take the Sabbath off. The Jewish leaders then tried to kill Jesus, because he broke the Law and declared that God was his Father, making himself equal to God.

After the Jewish leaders challenged Jesus, he answered them by saying that he couldn't do anything by himself. He said he could only do what he saw God do. In a real sense, Jesus was saying he copied his Father's methods. Then Jesus said that his Father loves him and shows him everything he does and will show him even greater things (to do) than he has already done. Now, here is where this starts getting interesting because it tends to suggest future events. Jesus said,

> **"… as the Father raises the dead and gives them life, even so the Son gives life to whom he is pleased to give it."**

This is an incredible statement. It shows that God has given or will give Jesus power of life and death – and it is beginning to sound like this power extends beyond the grave. But, before we get to that, we need to answer a bigger question: When did the Father raise the dead and give them life? Keep in mind that the Greek text is saying this is a continued action (not past). The Father "raises" the dead – not "raised" the dead. But, were there times, before Jesus was born, that God used his power to raise the dead? Was this a pattern of the Father? I think we can say, yes. There were three people raised from the dead that were named in the Old Testament. In addition to those named, others were raised who were not named. So, the Father displayed this power and ability, long before Jesus was born, and Jesus is copying his Father's character and actions.

Jesus also followed this statement with another that seemed outrageous to the Jewish leaders. He said that the Father judges no one but entrusts all judgment to the Son. Wow. Jesus was given the authority to judge all men. Maybe because he became a man, it only seemed fair that a perfect man judges the rest? Remember, too, that this word "judgment" is not an assessment of guilt or innocence, this is sentencing – it is condemnation.

Are you seeing ideas developing in this text, without outside influence or preconceived ideas? I hope so. Now consider this: Jesus goes on to say (verse 24) that whoever hears him and believes, will not be judged (condemned), but instead, will be offered life ("crosses over"). Then we come to our verse about the resurrection (verse 25) - or, is this about the resurrection? Hmm. If God the Father has given all judgment to Jesus, then it is Jesus who is deciding who will live and who will die. So, is this afterlife judgment or is this about the judgment of the Jews in 70 AD? Hmm. This is starting to sound like a mysterious science fiction episode, right? Well, what does verse 25 and 26 say and what do they not say? Let's look again.

"Very truly I tell you, a time is coming and has now come when the dead will hear the voice of the Son of God and those who hear will live. 26 For as the Father has life in himself, so he has granted the Son also to have life in himself."

As we look again at this passage, consider what Jesus said before this (verse 24):

"… whoever hears my word and believes him who sent me (God the Father), has eternal life and will not be judged …"

This looks like a connection to me. What do you say? This seems pretty clear when we do a Fresh-Read. If you hear Jesus' voice (believe what he says), then you will be granted life and not be condemned. Since no one may have been granted eternal life before this (at least those who were on planet earth at Jesus' time), then everyone Jesus talked to were "dead."   They were spiritually dead and since God is timeless, they were, to God, already dead in respect to the next life. They were bound for the "second death," which some scholars describe as eternal separation from God. Now, this calls for some research on your part, to determine what kind of death and life this is. Is it physical or a matter of the soul? Was it saving them from a tragedy on this earth, or was it escaping Hell – or was it maybe both?

I want you to notice one thing about this passage of scripture. So far in our reading, Jesus does not specifically say that those who hear his voice will "live again," as being raised from the grave." The text says those who hear his voice will live. Some

Eschatologists view this passage as Jesus calling people up from the grave. Now it is true that in verse 25, the people who hear Jesus' voice are "dead" – and it is true that those who are dead will "live" - but notice what Jesus said before this: "a time is coming and has now come." So, if the time when this occurs is a general resurrection of the dead, thousands of years in the future, how could it also have already come at Jesus' time? This requires research on your part and some careful reading of this text to make sure you are not making assumptions.

When we get down to the 28th verse, there are more details about the context of what Jesus is talking about. Let's see if the follow-up verses add more clarity.

John 5:28-30

> **"Do not be amazed at this, for a time is coming when all who are in their graves will hear his voice 29 and come out—those who have done what is good will rise to live, and those who have done what is evil will rise to be condemned. 30 By myself I can do nothing; I judge only as I hear, and my judgment is just, for I seek not to please myself but him who sent me.**

Okay, now we can see what Jesus is talking about. This "hearing his voice" must include a rising from the grave for all people, both good and evil." The good (believers) will rise to live and the evil will rise to realize their condemnation.

Now, we have a real problem and it is mountainous. If indeed this passage is about all people being called out of their graves and realizing their predetermined fate, then how could Jesus say the time for this occurrence had already started (verse 25)? Well, you must dig in and see what you can make of all this, but let me make a suggestion: In eschatology, I think we are in error when we are too ready to use lumped-in interpretations. Many end-times scholars want to say that because all people are going to hear Jesus' voice and be raised, all people must rise from their graves at the same time. This implies a mass grave exit (including those buried at sea, cremated, etc.) at the end of the world. But is this interpretation, forced by the text in John? Perhaps it may be in another scripture, but I am not at all sure we can force this meaning on this passage. For instance, if a person dies, then let's say shortly after death their soul is "called" from the "grave" and their soul either goes to live in Paradise with Jesus or is condemned to Hell, does this also satisfy the terms Jesus set out in this passage of scripture? Can each person's soul be judged from the time of Jesus forward, for thousands of years, without most of them having to wait until the end of time? Hmm. Well, toss that around in your head and read the text again. I just do not see a need to say all people rise at the same time or that hearing Jesus' voice from the grave is only one call. Maybe each person hears and each person responds, regardless of the time frame.

The Text, Next

We are moving along now, to the next passage, which is also in the book of John.

John 6:39

"This is the will of Him who sent me, that of all that He has given me I lose nothing, but raise it up on the last day."

Read it, read it, read it - fresh and new. It seems Jesus is recorded as saying that his Father's will is for him to hang onto all that has been given him. Was this the disciples, all the believers, all his power and authority – or all of the above? To determine this, we again must look at the surrounding text for clues, right?

John 6:35-40

35 Then Jesus declared, "I am the bread of life. He who comes to me will never go hungry, and he who believes in me will never be thirsty. 36 But as I told you, you have seen me and still you do not believe. 37 All that the Father gives me will come to me, and whoever comes to me I will never drive away. 38 For I have come down from heaven not to do my will but to do the will of him who sent me. 39 And this is the will of him who sent me, that I shall lose none of all that he has given me, but raise them up at the last day. 40 For my Father's will is that everyone who looks to the Son and believes in him shall have eternal life, and I will raise him up at the last day."

Perhaps adding these extra verses helps us to better understand what Jesus was trying to say. Read it straight and without bias, before trying to get the meat out of it. After you do, let's discuss it.

Let's see what we have here in the first part of this passage. Jesus said he is the "bread of life." It seems he is saying that he has a way of feeding us that gives us true life. This could be about eternal life as opposed to the temporary physical life we have here on this planet. Jesus, a life-giving Spirit, apparently can satisfy the hunger and thirst that exists in mankind – not just certain people. How do we know this? Because Jesus' statement had no caveats or prerequisites. It sounds like anyone could come to Jesus and get this bread of life. However, as Jesus goes on, he says that the people he is speaking to still do not believe in him. He adds that some do or will believe in him. He says that God his Father gives him some people and for those his Father gives him, Jesus will never drive away (or turn away). At least this is how I view this part of the passage. It seems fairly clear to me. Now, we can play with the semantics, assign a deeper meaning to the bread of life, and connect it with other scriptures that use the word bread, then create an elaborate lesson, but let's not. Let's just take this as Jesus said it and, as much as possible, let it stand on its own. We can also manipulate this and try to extrapolate meanings for "all the Father has given me," but taking this all in context, it seems pretty clear that Jesus is talking about those who believe in him as the Messiah and those who do not. Again, we are in a better position, theologically and apologetically, to take this passage at face value and not try to assign symbolism that may or may not apply; that may not have been intended by the writer.

We are now tackling the next part of this passage, beginning with verse 38. Read it over and see if there is any new information. I see that Jesus is proclaiming he came down from heaven and that he is performing the agenda of the one who sent him (his Father). After this startling news, he then says, that his Father's agenda is that he not lose the people his Father gave him. At this point, Jesus is, at least in part, referring to his disciples (other than Judas). Right after this, Jesus said he will "raise them up at the last day". This is an odd phrase because the "last day" is not defined and it is not a common term we use today. But, I want to come back to this in a minute. Looking at the rest of this passage, I see that Jesus is promising eternal life for everyone who "looks to the Son." Again, Jesus says that those who look to him, he will raise up at the last day. This is how I see it, but you may get something else from this passage.

There seems to be a theme here of Jesus having the God-given ability to keep his followers safe – at least in an eternal frame of reference. To me, this statement about not losing any that have been given him is based on the ability of Jesus to "raise them up." Now, is this resurrection from the dead or some other raising? It is hard to say for sure from this text. For one, we still don't know what this "raise them up" means or what "the last day" means. This requires some simple, yet possibly extensive searching to find meanings of the Greek text and other scripture that uses these terms.

I want to first tackle the phrase "raise them up." In Greek, the word sounds like "anestame." Unfortunately, it has various meanings. The most prominent idea seems to be "to stand up" or "be raised from a laying down position." It can be a raising up from the dead, or merely a raising up from a lying position. The word can also mean a person who is rising to challenge another or to kind of "stand forth" as a king or a prophet. This word can also be used to refer to a person who is about to enter into a dialogue or dispute. Thus the use of the word seems to be mostly a reference to "standing up" in a physical sense, or today's American terms, "standing up" to someone in a verbal and/or posturing way. Now, I would say that the way John uses the word in this context the meaning is not that disciples would be made to stand up to others. It is possible, but it seems this meaning of the Greek word, would be more applicable to voluntary action. If I am choosing to stand up to someone, then this meaning works, but I am not sure a writer would use this word, if he was meaning someone else is producing the power for someone to stand up, as in a challenge. So, in this case, as far as the Greek is concerned, I am going to side with the meaning that Jesus was probably talking about physical raising. Jesus could have been talking in symbolic terms and thus meaning the disciples would someday see their work and their Spiritual "cause" being put down and thwarted, then by the power of God, their cause is brought back to life. In my view, I think this is stretching the text and possibly manipulating it – or over-spiritualizing it. I think we should try to stick with the more simple explanation, that more likely than not, Jesus is referring to raising his disciples to everlasting life. This is also the classic interpretation of this text.

Now to the more problematic phrase "at the last day." In previous chapters, we had the challenge of trying to figure out a similar phrase "the end." We said in the case of "the end" that it was the end of a task of an event(s), and that it was not a matter of a certain amount of time passing. Thus, dates on the calendar were meaningless. When it was over, it was over. In the case of this phrase that John uses, "at the last day," it could have a similar meaning or it could be something completely different. I know many futurists seem to view this "last day" in the same way as "the end," but I am not sure these terms mean the same thing. First, let's go back to the Greek.

The Greek word for "last," sounds like "eskhatos." It is also a fairly flexible word and can mean last in time or place. It can refer to the last in a sequence of events or the last in a time sequence. It can also be used to refer to the extreme regions of the earth (the last place on the planet), or the last or lowest in rank. The simplest literal translation is probably "outermost."

Before we try to assign meaning, let's look at the word, "day." In Greek, the word sounds like "hamera." It very easily can be an actual 24-hour day, thus, having the same meaning as we use today, but it can also have some other meanings. It can mean a day that is in the light (as opposed to night), and it can mean a metaphoric day. If used metaphorically, it can refer to a period where wickedness is set aside (because evil is done in the dark). It can also mean the last day of a person's life. I think this may help us define the terms Jesus used. If the Greek text is saying that Jesus was given the power to raise his disciples to life on a specific day, then this makes perfect sense. It could be the last day of the world, the age, or after the disciples' tasks (which would have likely ended when they died). Now, if we don't get crazy here and move this event to the end of the world (doomsday), then we can see that the simplest explanation is that Jesus was able to raise those who had died and give them eternal life. It tends to lose idea flow, if we say that his followers were raised to physical life, then given eternal life. It just does not match the way this is stated in the sixth chapter of John. The "day" that is "last" is likely the last day of their life, not the last day of the age (also in keeping with one meaning of the Greek word).

Here is my logic – you can get your own if you like: If one meaning of the Greek word for "day" can be the last day of a person's life and John writes that Jesus said, "last day," it seems that John is re-enforcing the meaning of "day." We could say then, that in context, the word "last," before the word "day," narrows the various possible meanings. I suppose in a crude way we could say that John is writing this as "the very last day" of a person's life. It could very well be kind of redundant to make sure the reader understands the term means the last day of a person's life. Also since there are no other prophetic events mentioned; not plagues, wars, marching armies, etc., we can rightly assume that Jesus is not referring to the end of an age, the end of the judgment on Jerusalem, or any of the other things that come with troubled times that are talked about in Matthew, Mark, and Luke. Bottom line? I am going to say that "the end" is not the same concept as "last day." "The end," seems to be when the disciple's task of spreading the Good News is complete, whereas "the last day," seems more likely to be the day when Jesus' disciples die. Yes, it is possible, as I said, that the end of the disciples' task could be also the day they die, but the scriptures that talk about these subjects do not demand this meaning. The disciples' task could have ended before their death. However, the last day is the last day of life – if we are correct in our assessment of the terms. You will have to thoroughly research this, and look at other texts to see if our initial interpretation is right. It is from a Fresh Read, and its simplicity may be producing good things, but there may be other unseen factors that also need to be considered.

The Answer?

Okay, my friends, did we answer any questions about the dead raising and when? Hmm. Well, another text in John 6:54 uses similar terms, but I don't see any value in discussing it in this study. Please make sure you read it and see what you think. Overall, when looking at texts in the Gospel books about God raising people from the dead, I see no proof or substantial evidence that people who have died will be raised in a bodily form. It is still possible, but I see no text that seems to say this clearly. What I have seen, so far, is that people are going to be raised from their graves/death to immortal life and that the "when" seems to be on the day we die, not hundreds or thousands of years later. I also have not seen solid proof of Jesus taking dead people away in a mass exodus. Again, this could happen. I mean, God is God, and we need to let him be God, but I do not see the level of evidence in scripture that I would expect when it comes to a major doctrine. You run it out and see what you think. Just be careful not to connect dots that Bible writers may not have intended to be connected – and try hard not to manipulate the text to make it be what you want it to be. We are flawed. God's Word is not.

Chapter 11

Let's Eat!

I have noticed that in many churches, food is an important part of the social structure. A small country church near my home says they have food for all events – or at least this is the way it seems. I do know for a fact, they are a very "eating" church. I guess feasting makes for happy people because I have never met a nicer group of Christians.

However, I suppose there is always some sort of division about any subject in the Christian church. I imagine it happens in every secular club and organization, also. Someone once said opinions are like noses – everyone has one. Where there are opinions, there are also disagreements. Thus, there can be a debate about whether having a lot of food served in our church events qualifies as overindulgence or possibly even gluttony. Of course, Jesus and his disciples were accused of being or associating with gluttons and sinners, so I guess we are in good company (joking). Now, there is always a middle ground when it comes to things we enjoy, but on the flip side of this gluttony issue, it is important to see that fellowship in the church was encouraged and a very integral part of the early church. Christians often met together and possibly because of the culture, they broke bread and ate together. So, in all practicality, it seems very right and Biblical for the church to practice hospitality on all occasions. At the same time, it is also right for each believer to use restraint when it comes to how much they eat on these occasions.

Now, I hope you will excuse me, if I came across as preachy, I just wanted to make a point that leads to what we are studying next.

The Great Feast - Preface

Several scriptures talk about a great feast or banquet that is given in heaven, but before we start our text examinations, I think it is important for us to know one thing. In the orthodox Jewish faith, there is also a doctrine of a future feast. So, it is possible that what Jesus was talking about was foretold by prophets many years before Jesus was born.

Listen carefully: What I am about to reveal may violate RID rules. This information could taint your ability to truly read reference text in a Fresh Read manner. So, be cautious. If you do not believe you can set this information aside when reading the texts on Bible feasts, then skip over this section. Now, some readers may be asking why present this information if there is a risk of idea pollution. Here is my answer: Terms like the Great Feast or Banquet sound very generic and usually have little detail connecting to them in scripture. So when we read the associated Bible passages, we are going to mostly get muddy heads and questions about what Jesus is talking about. Yes, we have been down this kind of road and effectively resolved any issues after the text was read, but in this case, I think it is important to know where Jesus, and those who were listening, got their doctrine. We find this quite a bit in scripture. Many times the details are left out because the audience is well aware of what the teacher is referencing. If we know some things up front, then we can receive the Bible passages more like the hearers of Jesus' time. Having this mindset gives us an advantage in this case, and since the doctrines we are discussing in this chapter are not earth-shattering in eschatology, we are pretty safe exploring in this fashion, this one time.

Banquet Considerations

Feasts or banquets in Jesus' teaching often seemed to be connected to weddings. There are also a fair number of examples of wedding feasts in the Old Testament. In addition to the more passive examples, there is an interesting passage in Isaiah:

Isaiah 25:6-9

> **On this mountain the Lord Almighty will**
> **prepare a feast of rich food for all peoples, a**
> **banquet of aged wine- the best of meats and**
> **the finest of wines. 7 On this mountain he**
> **will destroy the shroud that enfolds all**
> **peoples, the sheet that covers all nations; 8 he**
> **will swallow up death forever. The Sovereign**

**Lord will wipe away the tears from all faces;
he will remove the disgrace of his people
from all the earth. The Lord has spoken. 9
In that day they will say, "Surely this is our
God; we trusted in him, and he saved us.
This is the Lord, we trusted in him; let us
rejoice and be glad in his salvation."**

You will want to do a Fresh Read on this, of course. When I read this, I get a strong impression that this is symbolic language. First, the idea that on any single mountain, food being served for every person on planet earth is just not possible or practical. The second most prominent thing I noticed is that this text very much sounds like a prophecy for when the Messiah comes. Many texts in Isaiah foretell the Messiah, and this one is viewed by many scholars as also being about him. It is very possible that Jesus was referencing himself and what he was going to do when he mentioned feast/banquets in his parables and other teachings.

In addition to this reference, Judaism sees the Sabbath as a celebration of the coming Messiah – as a bridegroom. We see this principle (in part) also in Isaiah.

Isaiah 58:13-14

**13 "If you keep your feet from breaking the
Sabbath and from doing as you please on my
holy day, if you call the Sabbath a delight
and the Lord's holy day honorable, and if
you honor it by not going your own way and
not doing as you please or speaking idle
words, 14 then you will find your joy in the**

Lord, and I will cause you to ride on the heights of the land and to feast on the inheritance of your father Jacob." The mouth of the Lord has spoken.

This sounds to me like an admonition to joyfully keep the Sabbath, without compromise. But, there is also a promise that if the Israelites keep it in this way, they will feast on the inheritance of their "father Jacob." In other words, I think this is referring to the promise God made to Jacob and possibly even goes back to the promises God made to Abraham. These would be the inheritance of the Promised Land, but also the security and prosperity that the Messiah would bring and would last forever.

Without going into other scriptures, I think you can see how Jews at Jesus' time, who were looking forward to the Messiah, thought in terms of these feasts and banquets that were connected with the Sabbath, weddings, and the coming Messiah.

Jesus' Words – Beginning

The big question we are dealing with in this chapter is whether there has been or will be a great feast or banquet held in heaven. Some scholars are emphatically for this doctrine, while others are just as vehemently against the idea. So, let's begin to look at some of what Jesus said about feasts and banquets, and how they may or may not apply to a heavenly banquet. Let's look first at texts in Matthew

Matthew 8:11-12

**"I say to you that many will come from east
and west, and recline at the table with
Abraham, Isaac, and Jacob in the kingdom of
heaven; but the sons of the kingdom will be
cast out into the outer darkness; in that place
there will be weeping and gnashing of teeth."**

What does your first and Fresh Read tell you? What I see is
Jesus telling his followers that there will be foreigners coming
to a banquet table in heaven, where they will eat with the very
founders of the Israel nation. This also reinforces what Jesus
said to the Sadducees about God being the God of the living,
not the dead (Matthew 22:32). Jesus said he is the God of
Abraham, Isaac, and Jacob, who were still alive, in God's eyes.
Their souls were with him. This is the way I view it in a Fresh
Read. Now, whether this reclining at the table with the
patriarchs is literal or figurative, is hard to say. This passage
seems somewhat symbolic overall. Though Jesus was able to
eat after his resurrection, I am not sure that an eternal soul
needs to eat earthly type food. Perhaps there is another kind of
source for nourishment in heaven that everyone enjoys
together, but we are not told about these things. We can muse
about Jesus being the Bread of life and wonder about the Spirit
of God being described as the Living Water, but in heaven, we
do not know much about this table that Jesus is talking about.
Could this be the same imagery that Isaiah talks about? Hmm.
There is some mystery, here, right?

Looking at the second half of this, I see a contrast between
those who are welcomed in, get to sit down, and enjoy the
"feast," and those who are not allowed to come in and dine
with the patriarchs. Those that are not allowed in, are "cast out

into the outer darkness." We are told that "in that place there will be weeping and gnashing of teeth." We discussed this earlier in this book, but let's review these terms since they are not very common to our current phrasing. When we read the phrase "weeping and gnashing of teeth," I think we can gloss over it and think that this is all about being in anguish. We might think a soul is in so much pain and/or sorrow that it is crying tears and its teeth are kind of chattering. However, the Greek term for this "gnashing of teeth," allows for more than suffering. This term also can involve angry outbursts. The word picture here is more likely a cursing of God. We may be able to relate to this idea when we consider that even in our current English language, there is a similar use of this term. If we say someone is gnashing their teeth at another person, it means they are very angry with them and are readily vocalizing their displeasure. The expressions are often accompanied by a variety of four-letter expletives. So, you can imagine what kind of curse words are being thrown at God by those who are tossed out of the kingdom. Ouch!

There are very big questions that arise when we consider the eschatological aspects of this passage. Some of them are: Is this place of outer darkness, Hell - or is this a place of anguish on this earth? Since Jesus is using a parable format for these statements, we have the symbolic aspect of this to deal with. Now, I need to say this rather emphatically: It is a grave error to take literally what Jesus says in parables. I know of many futurists, as well as many others, who want to assign literal meaning to parables, dreams, and visions. This is a mistake. We must always take what we read in the spirit of the way it was written. Thus, when we read this passage, terms like "outer darkness" could mean a lot of things. One thing seems pretty clear: There does seem to be a contrast between where the believers are, and where the unbelievers are. By taking solid Christian principles across the board (from scripture), we can rightfully say that where Jesus is, there is "light," and where he is not, there is automatic "darkness." This darkness also includes evil and everything that is not good.

A follow-up question about all this, might be: Where is this place of outer darkness? Well, I would say that since this is symbolic, it would not necessarily have to be a physical place. It could simply be outside the kingdom of God. Since, from an earthly view, this kingdom is not visible (Luke 17:20), to be in the kingdom or out of it does not require a person to be in any physical locality. Now, you can read over this passage and see what you think, but it seems Jesus may not be talking about people being in heaven, hell, or any other place - just in or out of the kingdom (as members).

There is one other aspect of this outer darkness we can talk about, but it may not necessarily apply. Here is the thought: When Jerusalem was destroyed in 70 AD, the Christians were saved when they fled to the mountains. The unbelievers stayed behind and let me tell you, that place was very "dark." Josephus writes about the horrors that took place in the city when it was under siege. While all these horrors were going on, the Jews were likely both crying out to God to help them and cursing him for their anguish. So perhaps both spiritually and tangibly, the unbelievers were in darkness and terrible anguish.

Now, let's revisit our original question. We don't want to be trailing off to other sidelines. So, can we yet answer what and when this banquet with the patriarchs occurs? Hmm. Well, Jesus does say this is a feast in the kingdom of heaven, right? So does this mean that it takes place, physically in heaven? Hmm. Well, Jesus indicated that people could be in his kingdom while they were on earth, so, it seems possible to fulfill the terms of this parable while still being on earth. But then, where would Abraham, Isaac, and Jacob be?   Perhaps this is symbolic as well, but there is a fair amount of weight in the language, indicating that a meal or fellowship is taking place where all are at the same place (table). So this sounds like a gathering together. We cannot be sure from just this one parable, but there is an allowance for either spiritual or physical togetherness. So, where does this put us? Actually in a good place. RID requires us to put this on the shelf for now. We can't be sure, from doing a Fresh Read, or from seeing some other texts, so we are not going to play God here and assign meaning that is not clear. Later, we may see other scriptures that shed more light on this banquet idea, but for now, we need to see the principle Jesus was talking about and leave the specifics to God.

King and Wedding Feast

We now come to what is deemed by some scholars to be one of the big examples of this feast idea. It is found in Matthew, chapter 22.

Matthew 22:1-14

> **Jesus spoke to them again in parables,**
> **saying: 2 "The kingdom of heaven is like a**
> **king who prepared a wedding banquet for his**

son. 3 He sent his servants to those who had been invited to the banquet to tell them to come, but they refused to come. 4 "Then he sent some more servants and said, 'Tell those who have been invited that I have prepared my dinner: My oxen and fattened cattle have been butchered, and everything is ready. Come to the wedding banquet.' 5 "But they paid no attention and went off--one to his field, another to his business. 6 The rest seized his servants, mistreated them and killed them. 7 The king was enraged. He sent his army and destroyed those murderers and burned their city. 8 "Then he said to his servants, 'The wedding banquet is ready, but those I invited did not deserve to come. 9 Go to the street corners and invite to the banquet anyone you find.' 10 So the servants went out into the streets and gathered all the people they could find, both good and bad, and the wedding hall was filled with guests. 11 "But when the king came in to see the guests, he noticed a man there who was not wearing wedding clothes. 12 'Friend,' he asked, 'how did you get in here without wedding clothes?' The man was speechless. 13 "Then the king told the attendants, 'Tie him hand and foot, and throw him outside, into the darkness, where there will be weeping and gnashing of teeth.' 14 "For many are invited, but few are chosen."

There is a lot of text here, so read through it and see what you think. When you compare this parable to the one we previously discussed, there seems to be similar language. In this case, however, instead of just a table where believers dine, this is a whole wedding feast. In this story, the king's son is about to be married. The king has a wedding banquet prepared and then invites people (likely family and friends), to come. Now, perhaps this is an odd practice to us, but the king even sends out servants to tell the people who were invited that it was time to come to the wedding feast. I am not sure about you, but I would be running there. Food! And lots of it! Okay, maybe this is why I am overweight. Maybe I like food just too much, but this is a king, and kings usually put out some excellent food, lots of it and a lot of variety. I would think anyone would want to be there. However, it seems in this story that none of them wanted to come (or at least the vast majority of them). So, what was the king supposed to do about this? Well, the food is getting cold and it is eventually going to spoil (no refrigeration), so he sends his servants out again and invites them all again and urges them to come. This sounds like a lot of social pressure to come, doesn't it? But, they still would not come. Now, you might see this differently, but it seems the people who were invited didn't have emergencies or other urgent business to attend to, they just didn't want to come to the king's house. If we look at this from a more distant viewpoint, we could easily get the idea that these people who were invited didn't like the king, and didn't want to be around him. It is equally possible that the people just didn't care. They wanted to do what they wanted and didn't want the king to impose on them to do things for him. Either way, this whole situation reeks of rude and ultra-selfish behavior. To top this off, the people who were invited seemed to become very angry with the servants who kept asking them to come to the banquet. They even beat and killed the servants. So, the king, having the authority of a king, stopped sending servants with invitations and instead sent his army to destroy them. It was life for life, as the Mosaic Law said.

Now, before we look at the meaning of this first part, let's look at the rest of the story. Since the banquet was already prepared, the king instructed his servants to go out to the common places and invite strangers. The servants obeyed the king and invited "both good and bad" strangers. This sounds like a disaster to me, but perhaps the idea was to give anyone a chance to act honorably. Regardless, the king's idea worked, because the wedding hall was filled. However, when the king comes in to see the new guests, he notices one man who did not have wedding clothes. Now, assuming these were all strangers, perhaps some very poor, and that they were invited to come in directly from the streets, I think we can safely assume that the custom was for the king to provide these wedding clothes. So this was not likely a matter of a person being unable to afford wedding clothes, it was a matter of a person refusing to wear what was provided for him. When the king asked him why he was not wearing the wedding clothes, he was speechless. Why was he speechless? Why didn't he reply that he could not afford fancy clothes? I think it was because he had no excuse for not putting on what was provided for him. So, guess what the king did? He tied him up and threw him out into the "darkness." Here we have the same picture as the former parable. There is a place outside of where the believers are (where the King is), where everyone else is. After the story is told, Jesus talks about the lesson. "Many are invited, but few are chosen." Perhaps we could also claim the reverse and say, many are invited, but few choose to be with the King.

Now that we have done a Fresh Read, let's see what else we can learn from this passage. Does this help further clarify what the banquet is and when it occurs? Hmm. I am going to say that I don't see any information here that determines a specific timeline or clear reference to future events that could nail down when this banquet is given or exactly what this banquet represents - other than a fellowship of the believers with Christ. To me, this seems to be more of a story about the people who willingly come into the kingdom of heaven, versus the people who refuse the invitation. Thus, the timeframe would be irrelevant in terms of eschatology. What I mean by this is that the lesson may not be about end times. It seems to be more about a theme of "accept Christ today, or perish." I see this more in the light of 2 Corinthians 6:2 "… now is the day of salvation." Perhaps you will make some different conclusions about this passage, or you may just say, I don't know what it means. This is all fine and good. The position of "I don't know" is better than assigning our own theories or conjectures.

Using our R.I.D rules, do you see any words or terms that are odd in this passage? I don't see much here that is odd or confusing. I suppose the wedding clothes could be a bit of a mystery. We could easily assign meaning to this, but perhaps Paul said it best when he wrote to the Galatians.

Galatians 3:27

"… for all of you who were baptized into Christ have clothed yourselves with Christ.

When we come to Christ and accept him into our lives as Lord and Savior - when we have a new birth - we are essentially clothed with his righteousness. Our sinful self is covered with the perfection of Christ. During this wedding feast, whatever grimy, dirty clothing the people off of the street were wearing would be covered by a nice, clean and new robe. In a social setting like a wedding feast, wearing this nice robe would have been considered a matter of respect for the bride and groom, their family, and all of the other guests. In a moral sense, we cannot carry our grimy sin into the kingdom of God. He is a righteous and Holy God and to be with him; to be in his kingdom, we must be clothed with Christ. Since this is a strong principle in the Word of God, this is likely the picture Jesus is painting here. However, there is always room for debate. So put on your apologetics hats and make sure of what you believe.

Comparison of Luke

Now, I do not want to spend a lot of time on this, but I think we would be remiss to ignore a similar parable in the Book of Luke. So, let's look at Luke and see how it compares to the parable in Matthew.

Luke 14:15-24

> **When one of those at the table with him**
> **heard this, he said to Jesus, "Blessed is the**
> **one who will eat at the feast in the kingdom**
> **of God." 16 Jesus replied: "A certain man**
> **was preparing a great banquet and invited**
> **many guests. 17 At the time of the banquet**

he sent his servant to tell those who had been invited, 'Come, for everything is now ready.' 18 "But they all alike began to make excuses. The first said, 'I have just bought a field, and I must go and see it. Please excuse me.' 19 "Another said, 'I have just bought five yoke of oxen, and I'm on my way to try them out. Please excuse me.' 20 "Still another said, 'I just got married, so I can't come.' 21 "The servant came back and reported this to his master. Then the owner of the house became angry and ordered his servant, 'Go out quickly into the streets and alleys of the town and bring in the poor, the crippled, the blind and the lame.' 22 "'Sir,' the servant said, 'what you ordered has been done, but there is still room.' 23 "Then the master told his servant, 'Go out to the roads and country lanes and compel them to come in, so that my house will be full. 24 I tell you, not one of those who were invited will get a taste of my banquet.'"

Once you have read this over, without any bias, compare the ideas and the text with the wedding banquet story in Matthew. Are there significant variances? I would say, yes. First, it is important to recognize that before this passage, Jesus was teaching about being gracious. In verses 12 to 14, he is recorded as having said this:

12 Then Jesus said to his host, "When you give a luncheon or dinner, do not invite your

**friends, your brothers or sisters, your
relatives, or your rich neighbors; if you do,
they may invite you back and so you will be
repaid. 13 But when you give a banquet,
invite the poor, the crippled, the lame, the
blind, 14 and you will be blessed. Although
they cannot repay you, you will be repaid at
the resurrection of the righteous."**

So, we can see the premise for Jesus' parable from what he was
saying before. Jesus was talking about giving without
expecting back and helping those who were poor and disabled.
After saying these things, someone who was eating with Jesus,
said, "Blessed is the one who will eat at the feast in the
kingdom of God." He was likely a Jew and possibly not even a
true believer in Christ and he was talking about this belief that
most Jews had about enjoying a feast in the kingdom of God. I
am assuming this refers to an event that is after death. It seems
to dovetail with the things Jesus said about eating with the
patriarchs, sometime in the future. Since the patriarchs had
died, this feast that was formerly mentioned (in another
passage) had to be after this life. If what was said in the
passage we are now studying, is referring to this same event,
then this feast in the kingdom of God is set to happen after
people die. You still need to research this to form a simple, yet
intelligent interpretation.

After this fellow diner commented on eating at a heavenly
feast, Jesus begins the parable of a great banquet. I think the
first thing to note about this parable is that it is not described as
a wedding banquet and there are no wedding robes given out.
However, this story does include guests that were invited and

the aspect of how the guests refused to come. In this story, we hear some of the excuses given for not coming. In the wedding feast parable (in Matthew), there are no excuses listed, but it is possible the excuses would have been similar, had Jesus named them in that parable. Who knows? Similar to the wedding feast parable, the servants tell their master that the invited guests are not coming. So, again, we see a master instructing his servants to go out into the streets and invite just anyone. In this parable, however, the poor, crippled, blind, and lame were invited. These were who many considered the "dregs" of their society. They were usually dirty, probably not very nice smelling, and had nothing to offer in return. There would be none of the traditional gifts from those who attended for the one sponsoring the banquet. Note that in the end, the servants had to go quite a distance to find enough people to fill the house.

One thing to notice here is that there is no talk of people being thrown into the darkness or of gnashing teeth. Jesus' final point was simply this: "Not one of those who were invited will get a taste of my banquet." I take this as meaning that none of the good things Jesus offered those who were invited, would be given them, even if they asked for them later. It was a one-time invitation and it had a time limit for acceptance. Like in this parable, both salvation from sin (for our souls), and the invitation to come into the kingdom of heaven and escape the coming physical judgment on Judea, had a time limit for those Jesus was speaking to. This is the way I see it, anyway.

Confer a Kingdom

We have just a couple more places to check to assess this feast/banquet situation. The first of them is in Luke 22.

Luke 22:29-30

> **"And I confer on you a kingdom, just as my Father conferred one on me, so that you may eat and drink at my table in my kingdom and sit on thrones, judging the twelve tribes of Israel."**

This passage is fairly short, so just look it over for a first impression. Here is how I assess this text: It seems a detail that is clear in several scriptures, but not talked much about, is that God the Father, "conferred a kingdom on Jesus. Now, this word, confer, is not a term we use much in today's English, but one dictionary describes this word as meaning, "grant or bestow." As I understand the meaning, it seems to be the same idea as when a person wills their property to their next of kin. So, in a sense, Jesus inherited a kingdom from his Father. Now, this was not passing on a kingdom because God was dead or dying, this was passing on an inheritance solely because of the Father's grace. What is surprising to non-theologians, is that Jesus turns around and wills his inherited kingdom to his followers. I guess this might be a little like some businesses today that are employee-owned. It appears to me, that Jesus then said that what came with this kingdom ownership, was the right to dine at Jesus' table in his kingdom. So, it sounds like this passing on of this kingdom might be more like adding owners, than transferring owners – which makes more sense. The Father may have passed this kingdom to Jesus, but at the same time, not taken his name off of the title. Then, when Jesus passed the kingdom to his disciples in the same way, their names were added to the title, along with the existing names of Jesus and the Father. Another perk of all this kingdom inheritance is that the disciples would receive thrones (symbolic of power and authority), and judge the twelve tribes of Israel. Now, this is some serious power and position. And, if you look up this Greek word for "judge," you will see that it sounds like "kreeno," and means this: to separate, put asunder; to pick out, select, choose; to approve, or esteem. So it sounds to me like this is not a condemnation type of judging. Many of the place in scripture where the Greek is translated as "judge" it is about a sentencing or final judgment, but here seems to be more like judging right from wrong. It may have to do with separating the good people from the bad as well, but it is not solely this type of action.

Okay, so does this help us know the when and how of feasts/banquets in the kingdom of heaven? Again, I say, hmm. It sounds to me like two events happen at the same time or they happen after a certain time. Why? Because they seem to be grouped. It might not necessarily be intentional by the writer, but it kind of seems that way to me. Let's read it again:

> **"… so that you may eat and drink at my table in my kingdom and sit on thrones, judging the twelve tribes of Israel."**

Seems to me that eating and drinking at Jesus' table are realized or given along with the right to judge. So the privileges are given at the same time. Perhaps this is the reason they are grouped.

The last question I have about this is "when do these things begin to take place?" If we can determine this, it may help resolve the "when" for the previous parables. To analyze this, we may not be able to go wholly to scripture – and this is unfortunate. We may, however, gain some insight by asking the negative or opposite questions. Sometimes when we use this kind of analysis, we don't get specific answers, but we get the parameters. These parameters tell us the framework these events are in, thus telling us what doctrines are not within the overall framework of the text. So, here are some questions we can ask: If there is any symbolic assignment or association to what Jesus was saying, when is the earliest possible time this could have been fulfilled? When did Jesus eat at a table with the disciples – and at a time when the disciples would have been considered to be "in the kingdom of heaven?"   Add to this another question: When were the disciples first given authority to judge Israel (or the people of Israel)?

Now, some scholars will claim that eating at a table with Jesus in the kingdom, was realized at the Last Supper. This is doctrinally possible, but there is some dispute about whether the disciples were in the kingdom or not at the Last Supper because they all abandoned him after that. So, your homework assignment is to look at the Bible text before and after the Last Supper text to see if there are any clues Jesus gave of when the disciples were officially "in the kingdom of heaven."

As far as ruling, and or judging the twelve tribes of Israel, this is often thought of by scholars as being more for the Day of Judgment in heaven. That is, they believe the disciples are ruling from heaven after their death. However, it is also possible that Jesus gave this authority to the disciples for use in their lifetime here on earth. After all, the disciples were the leaders of the church and had to settle many issues within the church (new bride of Christ). If, as is taught in the New Testament epistles, the believers are grafted in or adopted into the vine that used to be reserved only for Israel, and if Israel was rejected by God as a corrupt nation, and judged/cutoff, then the church, at least in the first century, would have been like a new Israel. The believing Jews and believing gentiles formed what would have been the new seed that God created for Abraham. If the construction of this reasoning is sound, then it is not beyond reason to deduce that the disciples were given the authority (thrones) to judge the new Israel. This puts the earliest possible fulfillment at shortly after Jesus' ascension.

Now, this kind of reasoning has much of its basis in scripture but is still stitching together texts that may or may not have been desired by the Bible writers. So, we can speculate and wonder. We may even form personal beliefs, but we cannot teach these things as absolute facts unless we can show solid scripture that is irrefutable. Thus, we must admit in the end, that it is possible for this text in Luke to be fulfilled during the disciples' life or after they are in heaven. There may be no absolute proof, at least not from this one text. I suggest you scholars do a check in the Book of Revelation to see about who is ruling in heaven.

The Issue of the Cup

We now come down to the last passage we are going to consider in our quest for answers to this feast and banquet quandary.

Matthew 26:27-29

> **Then he took a cup, and when he had given thanks, he gave it to them, saying, "Drink from it, all of you. 28 This is my blood of the covenant, which is poured out for many for the forgiveness of sins. 29 I tell you, I will not drink from this fruit of the vine from now on until that day when I drink it new with you in my Father's kingdom."**

There is a lot of meat in this passage, so read it carefully, while not interjecting thoughts, at this point. What did Jesus say, and what did he not say? This happens during the Last Supper. Jesus picks up the chalice and tells them all to drink from it. This was a custom in their day, where a group of close friends or relatives would show their respect for their relationship and pledge their loyalty to each other by drinking from the same cup. Of course, the knowledge of germs was not yet known, so this did not bother any of them. Jesus then declared that this cup and the wine that was in it was the "blood of the covenant." He said it was poured out (or possibly it was going to be poured out), for many to provide forgiveness of sins.

Then Jesus says something a little perplexing to us in the 21st century. He said he would not drink from this wine until he drinks it with them in his Father's kingdom. The big question here is this: Is this drinking with them going to be on earth or after they die? Is this a reference to the great banquet with Jesus and the patriarchs? Hmm. Well, it certainly is not very clear, because Jesus did not give us very many details. I am sure the disciples now know what Jesus was meaning, but I am pretty sure they did not know what he meant at the Last Supper. So, your assignment is to run this out. Do some searches in the Bible, and compare drinking of wine and references to the "cup," to see if you can find any link or similar images that help explain this scenario.

One thing we can consider in all this is that after Jesus rose from the dead and visited the disciples, he did eat and drink with them. I think we can safely say that by the time Jesus rose from the dead, the kingdom of heaven was in full operation and Jesus was fully in power as its King (if he somehow was not before). Here is what Peter said in Acts 10

Acts 10:39-41

> **"We are witnesses of everything he did in the country of the Jews and in Jerusalem. They killed him by hanging him on a cross, 40 but God raised him from the dead on the third day and caused him to be seen. 41 He was not seen by all the people, but by witnesses whom God had already chosen—by us who ate and drank with him after he rose from the dead.**

It certainly sounds like Jesus ate and drank with the disciples after he arose. Your task is to determine whether this fulfills what Jesus prophesied.

Summary

So, did we resolve any of the questions surrounding the "what and when" of these heavenly feasts or banquets? Possibly.

Some references seem to be connected with some Old Testament scriptures that were already embedded into the Jewish faith (as prophecies). Others could be symbolic of events that happened within the lifetime of the disciples. I must say after much study, that there is hardly a slam dunk for one doctrine or another. Maybe, in the end, it does not matter. These prophecies seemed to be targeted mostly at the disciples, not us. They may affect us, but if they do, we do not need to worry about them or worry about whether we are having "faith" for them to happen. Whether we have faith or not about these feasts or banquets, God will carry them out just as he planned, and in the time frame of his choosing. Some things may have already occurred. After all, the disciples have been with Jesus for a very long time. There has been a lot of time for them to sit down and dine with the patriarchs. If we are not selfish in eschatology and think that everything is about us, then we can concede that even a Great Banquet for the disciples could have occurred. There may be more than one feast in heaven, who knows for sure? Check it out for yourself, my dear friend.

Chapter 12

What about Israel?

Mrs. Dent loved to give the best birthday parties in the county. There seemed to be no end to what this lady would do to make the biggest, brightest, and most entertaining parties. There would often be bouncy houses, clowns, and magicians. The decorations were colorful and elaborate – and when it came to food, my-oh-my, there was always enough to feed an army. When it came to gifts, no other parent could compete. The birthday boy or girl would have a big pile, but it didn't stop there. Every guest received a gift when they arrived and had opportunities to gain more throughout the time of the party. One year, Mrs. Dent put out a set of tables that was about 12 feet long and piled it with every toy that a child could want. When the guest children arrived, she told them they could pick any gift on the table they wanted, but they could only have one. You can imagine the mayhem that ensued. Now, this seemed on the surface to be a very generous and good thing to do, but to many of the children, it was almost cruel. Some of the children that attended came from very poor families and they saw their wildest dream piled on those tables. Half of the toys there had been their dream to obtain, yet they could only pick one. Many of the children were emotionally torn, and a few of the children had a terrible time trying to decide which toy to keep. What was meant with love and grace, became a frustration, and even a couple of tears for young children. I'm not sure we would classify this as a tragedy, but it was certainly a bump in the road for an otherwise successful party.

Concerning things we can obtain in this world, it is not easy to choose the best. Sometimes, we pick the right thing, and other times we pick things that are very bad for us. I suppose this is also true in Bible studies – and especially in eschatology. Now, some readers might ask, how can this be? Here is my answer: In every chapter, every verse, and every phrase, we have to make a choice. The choice is always how to take what is presented. Just as when you are having a conversation with someone and how you hear them is based on your current mood, our moods can affect how we receive what we read in God's Word. If we are very happy, we will look at a text with a positive and hopeful attitude. If we are upset, angry, or sad, then we may read Biblical text with disdain, or adopt a doomsday interpretation. Choosing the best and most accurate meaning is so very important, yet at times, also very difficult. As we move through this chapter, remember that how you view things in the Bible can easily be tainted by previous influences, your general outlook on Christianity, your personal experiences, and your current mood. Try very hard to stay objective and not take sides. When we become blind to others' opinions and believe we have all the right answers, we stop learning. When we stop learning, we stop growing. The truth is, there is always more to see and learn from the Bible. We will never know all there is to know. In fact, it seems to be God's plan for our lives to reveal only small portions at a time. If we allow God's Holy Spirit to lead us and guide us, he will show us marvelous things. And, while we are learning and growing, what we hold as "right doctrine" may be completely tossed out the window someday. And these growth changes that God may take you through, will not likely be because someone persuaded you to believe differently. It will be because the Spirit of the Living God, revealed something in his Word in a way you had never seen before. This being said, those huge changes will be infrequent, not every day. Most of what we know and believe will be proven, over and over. If you are a fundamental Christian, then the core of what you believe should be unshakeable. What you believe about eschatology, however, can be challenged. Why? Because God has not revealed all of it to any one person. Much of our future is veiled, and no one, but no one, knows for sure how or when this world will end.

About Israel – the Beginning

We have now studied most of the more prominent prophetic words of Jesus. There is just one more area I want to look at. It is a highly controversial area of eschatology and it has to do with the role of Israel in the end times. There are a couple of classic views, so let me put these out on the table for your perusal.

One popular view is that Israel is central in end-times prophecy and that they will remain that way to the end. The other view is that Israel plays no role as a nation in end-time prophecies. Now, there are varied views under each of these "sides." I could be wrong, but after seeing countless commentaries and many views of eschatology, I believe the core issue about Israel is whether God has and will always favor her as a nation and as a people and deal with her the same way he did in the Old Testament, or whether Israel turned their back on God (as a nation and a people), and God rejected them – then took up a new bride, which is the church. Thus, we must ask this all-important question: Is the body of Christ (made up of believing Jews and gentiles), essentially the new Israel in God's view? Did Israel give up her role as God's bride and did the church step into that role? There are both good, and yet tough, questions here. One thing we need to look into is the term "Israel Only." This is a term that majorly separates views in eschatology. And, believe me when I say that people become very angry over it.

First Step

Rather than trying to decipher all the ins and outs of "Israel Only," and similar issues, let's look at some scripture and see if we can lay down some basics about the nation of Israel, the Jews, and the church. The main question I want to address in this chapter is the one Jesus' disciples asked him: When will the kingdom be restored to Israel? Of course, we need to ask some other questions in our generation: Was the kingdom of Israel restored? If not, will it ever be restored?

To see the lay of the land on this subject, let's first look at the first chapter of Acts. The events in this passage occur after Jesus has risen from the dead.

Acts 1:6-7

**6 Then they (disciples) gathered around him
(Jesus) and asked him, "Lord, are you at this
time going to restore the kingdom to Israel?"
7 He said to them: "It is not for you to know
the times or dates the Father has set by his
own authority.**

Now, take a fresh look at this text and see what you think. This
meeting between Jesus and the disciples includes them asking
Jesus whether he was going to restore the kingdom to Israel.
To understand what this truly meant, we have to put ourselves
in the shoes of the disciples. The nation of Judah (not Israel),
was not an autonomous nation. It was under the rule of the
Romans. Judah had not been an independent nation for a long
time. They were conquered and enslaved as a people, because
of their constant rebellion against God, and their refusal to
obey his Law. The nation had practiced wicked things for a
very long time. In addition, the northern kingdom of Israel had
been obliterated. This is from Wikipedia, and it fairly well
sums up what we know from Biblical text.

**This is traditionally dated between 1050 BC
and 930 BC. On the succession of Solomon's
son, Rehoboam, around 930 BCE, the biblical
account reports that the country split into
two kingdoms: the Kingdom of Israel
(including the cities of Shechem and
Samaria) in the north and the Kingdom of
Judah (containing Jerusalem) in the south.**

Now, around 720 BC, the northern kingdom of Israel (the nation that was called Israel), was invaded by Assyria and the remaining population was deported. It does not appear (from what I could see) that the northern kingdom was ever restored. In Jesus' time, the southern kingdom, Judah, did have a native populous. The area was generally known as Judea. There are a lot of details about the split of Israel into two kingdoms, but both of the kingdoms were eventually conquered, and both went into captivity. But, only the southern kingdom was ever rebuilt, and at least had some self-rule. This has been a mystery to me for a very long time. If the kingdom of Israel had not been around for over 700 years, then why did Jesus' disciples ask if the kingdom was going to be restored? Was their belief that when the Messiah came, he would restore and unite both of the kingdoms that were split so long before – or did the Jews of disciple's day consider Judea to be "Israel?" Judah was a child of Israel (Jacob), so it might not have been wrong to call Judea, the land of Israel. I just hate to say it, but I don't know. There does not seem to be enough evidence in the Word of God to truly tell us how the disciples viewed Judea and the old kingdom that had once been in the north. You may need to look into historical records or information from Judaism, to find helpful input.

Getting back to this passage in Acts, let's see how Jesus answered:

> **(Jesus said), it was not for them to know the times and dates (of God's plans).**

Now, when we read this and other passages with a similar format, we need to be extremely careful. There has been a lot of eschatological wrenching on this scripture. So, let's look at it again with a magnifying glass. What we need to determine is what this text says and what it doesn't. Does Jesus say that the kingdom will be restored to Israel? I don't see that in Jesus' answer. It could include this aspect, but the stark reality of Jesus' answer is that he basically told them it was none of their business – it was his Father's business, alone (and God the Father wasn't telling).

What I find interesting about Jesus' answer is that it mirrors the mannerism he had adopted with his disciples when they once asked him about the end of their lives. Let's look at that scripture so you can see this parallel mannerism.

John 21:18-23

8 Very truly I tell you, when you were younger you dressed yourself and went where you wanted; but when you are old you will stretch out your hands, and someone else will dress you and lead you where you do not want to go." 19 Jesus said this to indicate the kind of death by which Peter would glorify God. Then he said to him, "Follow me!" 20 Peter turned and saw that the disciple whom Jesus loved was following them. (This was the one who had leaned back against Jesus at the supper and had said, "Lord, who is going to betray you?") 21 When Peter saw him, he asked, "Lord, what about him?"

22 Jesus answered, "If I want him to remain alive until I return, what is that to you? You

> **must follow me." 23 Because of this, the**
> **rumor spread among the believers that this**
> **disciple would not die. But Jesus did not say**
> **that he would not die; he only said, "If I want**
> **him to remain alive until I return, what is**
> **that to you?"**

Can you see the similarity here? Peter was told by Jesus how he would die. When Peter asked Jesus about John, Jesus said, it was none of his business. What he added was part of Jesus' position that Peter had no right to know how John would die. Jesus said, "If I want him to remain alive until I return, what is that to you?" The Bible text here, conveniently spells this out and says that many people believed John would not die, and spread rumors to this effect, but the text says that Jesus did not say this. If we visit what seems to be a similar scenario in our passage in the Book of Acts (chapter 1), we can easily see, without manipulating the text, that Jesus is telling his disciples it is none of their business. Because Jesus did not say the kingdom would not be restored to Israel, we cannot assume that Jesus meant it would be. The yes or no to this query was solely in the hands of God the Father – and this was Jesus' only point. So, please do not let anyone influence you to interject something that is not in this text (Acts 1:6-7). Jesus did not, in any way, promise or predict the kingdom would ever be restored to Israel (or to Judah).

Other Considerations

Israel Only

This is a general description of the doctrine of "Israel Only)":

**Israel-Only (IO) doctrine limits the audience
to physical descendants of Abraham and has
the eschatological events ALL fulfilled to,
with, and for them.**

In contrast, most Christian churches today, believe that many doctrines, instructions, and prophecies in the Bible include the gentiles also. So, if you wish to run this to the ground, then do some research for scriptures that may be used to support this doctrine, and weigh them to see if they have any merit. I think you may find some serious holes in this view, but you be the judge. Here are some scriptures to consider:

Matthew 5:17; Psalms 137; Isaiah 45:17; Romans 11:25-32; Isaiah 59:20-21; 27:9; Jeremiah. 31:33,34;

<u>Replacement</u>

Replacement doctrine can be described this way:

> **Replacement theology (also known as
> supersessionism) essentially teaches that the
> church has replaced Israel in God's plan.
> Adherents of replacement theology believe
> the Jews are no longer God's chosen people,
> and God does not have specific plans for just
> the nation of Israel.**

What do you think of this doctrine? Can it be true? Is it a slam dunk, Biblically? You will need to do some serious homework here. Regardless of your personal beliefs or what you have been taught, you absolutely must prove your viewpoint, beyond reasonable challenge. You must provide rock-solid scripture, without any fancy manipulation. The texts must be clear in their message. Here are some scriptures to consider in your research:

Romans 2:28-29; Philippians 3:3; Galatians 6:15-16: John 3:16; John 14:6; Jeremiah 31:31 + Hebrews 8:6-13; Romans 7:1-7; 1 Corinthians 3:16; 6:19-20; Acts 15:1-3; Gal 3:28-29

Any Others?

Before we leave this subject, you may also want to look at scriptures like these:

Genesis 49:10

> **The scepter will not depart from Judah, nor
> the ruler's staff from between his feet, until
> he to whom it belongs shall come.**

Isaiah 9:7

> **Of the greatness of his government and peace
> there will be no end. He will reign on David's
> throne and over his kingdom, establishing
> and upholding it with justice and
> righteousness from that time on and forever.
> The zeal of the LORD Almighty will
> accomplish this.**

Do you see any important information here? I think it is good to note that there is a strong theme in the Old Testament about the Messiah coming and taking charge of the nation of Israel. In prophecy, when he takes this throne, it will be forever. No other king will ever sit on the throne. Once the Messiah takes this permanent leadership, the nation of Israel will be established forever. Of course, there were always caveats to God's promises. The nation of Israel had to obey God and follow his Laws. If they did not, they would experience a lot of bad things and could even be blotted out of God's plan.

One other thing we need to consider is that in the Old Testament when Israel (or Judah) was being punished, a lot of Israelites died. So, when God allowed the nation to come back together and a government was reformed, the majority of the people who had been there before did not return. Only a remnant of the nation was saved. When Paul talks about the Jews, he also talks about God saving a remnant (Romans 11:5). So, we can rightfully say this: If any of the children of Israel remained when the Messiah (Jesus) came, took the eternal throne, and saved the remnant (that decided to finally obey God by accepting the Messiah and believing in him), then God's promise was fulfilled. The majority of Israel did not have to be saved for the prophecy to be fulfilled.

Perhaps the last question here is this: Who was and still is the King of Kings and Lord of Lords? Jesus, and no other. His kingdom was established and still stands. It is a permanent throne and a permanent kingdom. Guess who is in this kingdom and protected by it? All the children of Israel, who accept Jesus as the Christ. So, was the kingdom restored to Israel? In one sense and perhaps in the most important sense, yes. It was not like the old kingdom. The old kingdom of Israel fell, over and over again. The new kingdom of Israel under Christ had to be rebuilt on a different foundation and with different principles for it to stand for eternity. This should be the focus of the questions and the answers. All the other questions about Israel Only or Replacement doctrines may seem to have some merit in scripture, but neither of these is all that important. What is key is what the Bible says about Jesus and what he did, period. Everything else seems to just muddy the water of what Christ was truly about.

Chapter 13

Words of Apostles

Sound bites have become a plague in America and around the world. We have this "wonderful" technology that can capture what someone says, any place and any time, then play it back when it is convenient – or inconvenient. Powerful people, politicians, elected officials, movie stars, rock stars, and CEOs, have been quoted by the news media, competitors, and special interest groups. Sometimes these sound-bite quotes have been used to shed a light on heroism in these people. At other times, they have been used to destroy people's careers - and often their lives.

The very nature of sound bites is troublesome. It is the very essence of taking things out of context. A sentence or phrase taken from the middle of a long statement may or may not be true, by itself. In fact, if a person, while speaking about a certain subject, brings up the negative aspects of the subject, a sound bite of just the negative statements can easily be used to suggest the speaker is standing against the issue instead of for it. I sincerely doubt that any of us would like everything we say recorded. And, I think we would find it even more appalling to have short clips of what we say played back to others.

Since we find sound bites a bit disturbing (especially if we are the ones who are being recorded), I wonder why we play the sound-bite game with Bible book writers. For instance, if Doctor Luke were your friend today, would you like it, or even think it was appropriate if people in your neighborhood were repeating things he said, out of context, then claiming this was Luke's position or teaching? Hmm. I don't think so – and yet, the Bible writer "Luke" is your fellow brother in Christ. He is a currently living soul, the same as Abraham, Isaac, and Jacob, whom Jesus claimed were alive. So I suppose this sounds a little preachy, but we need to have respect for the Bible writers and protect what they penned. We need to not twist or manipulate what they wrote, and we need to keep their words in the context of what they wrote. If one of the writers is exhorting on a particular subject matter, then let's not take a verse from the middle of the passage, and claim it is different - then build a whole doctrine around that one verse. If it is not the subject matter the writer is speaking on, then it is a sound bite, taken out of context. And, yes, this technique is used every day to forward certain doctrines that are more likely man's theories than actual Biblical teaching.

Preface

As the last study of this book, we are going to look into some of the prophetic words of the Apostles. Since the Apostles learned from Jesus and taught others, we may get more insight into Jesus' words, by investigating what the Apostles were writing to the early churches.

Diving into the Deep End

Perhaps the most controversial eschatological doctrine is the "Rapture." The Greek word sounds like "harpazo," and it means to be caught up, or to be carried away. This is the belief that when Jesus returns he will first gather the believers who are living and dead and take them up to be with him in the clouds. More times than not, this is a secret coming that happens in the time it takes for an eye to twitch, or "twinkle." There are several verses used to support this doctrine, so we can't deal with all of them in this book. Note, however, that many of them can be interpreted in different ways and do not contain text that is specific to being taken away into the heavens. Of course, you will need to do some research on this subject yourself and look at each supporting verse to analyze them. Just don't go in with ideas either for or against them. Simply read the verses and see what they actually say and what they do not. Also, reference some of my comments in my other book, REVELATION WITHOUT INFLAMMATION. One thing I said there, was that Revelation was not a good book to support the Rapture doctrine. When reading it straight, without manipulation, that study showed there was only one verse in the entire book that plainly talked about "Rapture." That is, the Greek Word referencing Rapture, "harpazo" was only used when the two witnesses who had been slain were caught up to heaven. There is no other place in Revelation that talks about anyone being caught up to heaven, and certainly there are no masses that are specifically caught up to heaven – at least in these terms, or including the use of the Greek word.

Going Deeper

Let's dig into the subject of Rapture a little deeper. From my research and the lectures I have heard, it seems that there are three main scripture passages in the New Testament that are used for this doctrine. One of them is listed below.

1 Thess. 4:13-18

Brothers and sisters, we do not want you to be uninformed about those who sleep in death, so that you do not grieve like the rest of mankind, who have no hope. 14 For we believe that Jesus died and rose again, and so we believe that God will bring with Jesus those who have fallen asleep in him. 15 According to the Lord's word, we tell you that we who are still alive, who are left until the coming of the Lord, will certainly not precede those who have fallen asleep. 16 For the Lord himself will come down from heaven, with a loud command, with the voice of the archangel and with the trumpet call of God, and the dead in Christ will rise first. 17 After that, we who are still alive and are left will be caught up together with them in the clouds to meet the Lord in the air. And so we will be with the Lord forever. 18 Therefore encourage one another with these words.

So, what do you think? Does this sound like a secret return of Jesus, where he catches everyone away to heaven? Maybe so. Hmm. Let's analyze this text from the beginning and try to keep the ideas in the order Paul presents them.

First, note that Paul is answering a concern that the church in Thessalonica had. What seemed to be the concern or question? Well, Paul wrote, "… we don't want you to be uninformed about those who sleep in death, so that you do not grieve like the rest of mankind, who have no hope." So, this sounds like there was a question about believers who had died. Perhaps, because they had died before Jesus had returned there was a concern that only believers who were alive were going to be "saved," or be with Jesus. We don't know for sure what Paul was asked, so we just have to deduce.

When we get to the first part of Paul's answer, we see this:

> **"14 For we believe that Jesus died and rose again, and so we believe that God will bring with Jesus those who have fallen asleep in him."**

Now, what does this mean to you, in plain terms? It seems Paul is using the example of Jesus dying, then rising from the dead as a pattern for what believers will be doing. So, the first part of this verse seems fairly clear, but what follows seems to trip up a lot of scholars. Note the language Paul uses. He basically says this:

> **Thus, we believe that God will bring the dead believers with Jesus.**

So, here is my question: What does bringing them "with Jesus" mean? When we just read this straight, I have to ask, how can I make a case for the believers being caught up to meet Jesus, if the text says the dead believers are going to come "with" Jesus? This sounds to me like those who have died are going to accompany Jesus when he returns. So, what do you think? Again, I am not trying to make doctrine here, I am just trying to read it the way it is written.

Our next challenge is in verse 15.

> **15 According to the Lord's word, we tell you that we who are still alive, who are left until the coming of the Lord, will certainly not precede those who have fallen asleep.**

Here it sounds like Paul is continuing to try to calm the worried people in the church. He points out it is not him who is making this promise – it was the Lord himself that said, the believers who are still alive, when the Lord returns, will not precede those who have died. Of course, if the dead are going to be coming with Jesus, then those who are alive could not go ahead of them, to be with him. At least, this is what seems to make sense, given just the text we have read, so far. Of course, things could change in the text that follows, so we need to be careful about making any hard decisions about the overall meaning, yet.

Getting down to the 16th verse, we are going to see how it fits with what was in the former verses.

> **16 For the Lord himself will come down from heaven, with a loud command, with the voice**

**of the archangel and with the trumpet call of
God, and the dead in Christ will rise first. 17
After that, we who are still alive and are left
will be caught up together with them in the
clouds to meet the Lord in the air. And so we
will be with the Lord forever. 18 Therefore
encourage one another with these words.**

So far, in this complete passage, we have these two basic ideas:

1. The dead will come with Jesus (sounds like when he returns)

2. The living will not be with Jesus before the dead.

We need to make sure that we do not completely eject these premises in the text, while we add the remaining information. So, what does this text (from verse 16) say? Seems that Paul is saying Jesus will come down from heaven with the voice of the archangel (this sounds like war), and with the trumpet call of God. Note that trumpets were used to signal troop advancement – among other things. From our former studies of what Jesus said about his return, we could connect this passage with Jesus coming on the clouds to judge Israel. This does seem like an aggressive posture for Jesus in this passage we are studying. The next phrase can throw a lot of scholars off, because it says, "… and the dead in Christ will rise first." Now, a very normal reaction to this verse is to view this rising of the dead as being a nearly simultaneous event. It very well can be, but my question is this: Does it have to be a nearly simultaneous event to satisfy the Greek text?   If the dead have already gone to be with the Lord years before, would it also satisfy the meaning of this scripture? If Paul is still reinforcing his earlier message in this passage, then isn't it just as likely that he is merely reviewing his former statement? After all, the topic here is, Will the living believers precede those who are dead? The phrase in verse 16 is "the dead in Christ will rise first." When I read this, I say to myself, yes, of course, they rise first – they had to because they are coming "with" Jesus, right? Hmm.

Now, let's start piecing this puzzle together with the rest of the text. From verse 17

> **17 After that, we who are still alive and are left will be caught up together with them in the clouds to meet the Lord in the air. And so we will be with the Lord forever.**

Without making the verse something else, it seems that Paul is saying that the believers who are still alive, when Jesus returns, will be caught up together with the dead believers to meet with Jesus in the clouds – in the air. Hmm. This sounds again like the dead and living will meet in the air, then join Jesus. But this is because the phrasing in Greek is not the same as in English. This can also be translated as the living believers are caught up to meet the dead believers in the sky, who are already with Jesus. The meeting is in the clouds and with the Lord. So, it is rallying. Then we will all be together with Jesus, forever.

We have some issues here because this scenario does not exactly match what Jesus said about his return. When we read Jesus' words, straight, without manipulating them, there didn't seem to be a catching up of believers. And I don't know about you, but whenever there is a seeming discrepancy in the Bible,

I will take Jesus' words as the steering text to define all the others.

Here is possibly an alternate way to look at this text. Since Paul is trying to quell some fears in the church, he is making a case for all believers, both dead and living, to be with Christ for eternity. This is the core of his message to the Thessalonian church. So, let's back away from the text for a minute and view it in a different light. Then we can see if it is an honorable interpretation or questionable. Trumpets were not only used for a call to war, but also at funerals. What if Paul was referring to the last trumpet a person would hear (metaphorically) when they were in the grave, or about to be put in their grave? This last call by the trumpet also acted as a call for their spirit to leave their body and be with Christ. Then later, when the currently living died, they would get a trumpet call for them to go to be with Christ. As we have asked before: Is it necessary that all the dead and all the living go to be with Jesus at the same time? If so, this violates other texts that say when we are absent from the body, we are present with Christ - like the thief on the cross. Reference these texts for Paul's teaching: Philippians 1:23 & II Corinthians 5:8.

So we have quite a quandary here. Is this passage about a secret coming? Well for one, it doesn't seem very secret or very fast. Did the living believers go to be with Jesus and the dead believers, when Jesus came to judge Israel? Or is this language Paul is using to describe Jesus' gathering of the living believers in the mountains (up in the clouds)? The bottom line here is that there are way too many questions about this passage to say this is a slam dunk for Rapture doctrine. Still, it can rightfully be used in apologetics to support Rapture doctrine, because there is no solid way to say that a scholar has no right to view the verse in their way.

John's View

Let's take a look at some verses in John, chapter 14, verses 1-14, that are used for Rapture doctrine. I am not going to list them here, because it is a lengthy text and you have the tools to look this up and study it yourself, now. Here is how I read this passage. Jesus is telling his disciples he is going away and preparing a place for them and he will come back to receive them. Now, there is no specific talk of Rapture here or anything that sounds like Jesus is planning a group exit of all believers. I just want to make an important point here. These things were said and promised to the disciples, primarily – not to us. So, either Jesus fulfilled his promise to them, or he was a liar. I am sticking with the first answer. We saw in our study, how all that Jesus told the disciples about their future came true. We know the disciples all went to be with Jesus and dwell in the place he prepared for them. When we see these deeper truths, we need to adjust our doctrine to form around what all the prophetic texts say, as a whole.

Back to Paul

The last passage we need to look at is in first Corinthians 15.

I Cor. 15:50-58

50 I declare to you, brothers and sisters, that flesh and blood cannot inherit the kingdom of God, nor does the perishable inherit the imperishable. 51 Listen, I tell you a mystery: We will not all sleep, but we will all be changed— 52 in a flash, in the twinkling of an eye, at the last trumpet. For the trumpet will sound, the dead will be raised imperishable, and we will be changed. 53 For the perishable must clothe itself with the imperishable, and the mortal with immortality. 54 When the perishable has been clothed with the imperishable, and the mortal with immortality, then the saying that is written will come true: "Death has been swallowed up in victory."

Go ahead, and look over this text to see what you think – after a Fresh-Read. The first thing I see is that Paul is saying our physical bodies cannot own (or be part of?) the kingdom of God. It seems the reasoning is that what is mortal cannot obtain what is immortal. This leads me to think that there is no amount of effort or power in the flesh that can earn or deserve what is spiritual/eternal. Paul then says he wants to tell the church a mystery. So, let's stop here and consider how he is prefacing the statement that followed. He is telling them right up front that what he wants to tell them is mysterious. So, how should we read what follows? It seems what we read next is veiled. It is likely going to be something that the early church did not and could not fully understand. It was something that Paul received from the Lord, but even he did not fully understand it. Let's remember that for a person to relay a prophecy from God, they do not necessarily have to understand it. This is true of all of the prophets of the Old Testament as well. I am sure when the Old Testament prophets told of future events, they did not understand every detail that was going to happen. God kept those details to himself. So, as we read through this next part of the passage, there may be some things that are not obvious. And, according to our study rules (RID), we must not play God and assign meaning that is not in the text.

Here is the mystery: Paul says they will not all sleep. Note that he did not say everyone in the future generations. He was talking about himself and the believers that were alive at that time. I do not believe that God had revealed things to Paul about future generations at least at the point of Paul's writing. Now that we have this perspective, let's look at the rest of his statement. Paul says they would all be changed and that it would happen immediately. So lets' consider this mysterious statement. In what context is Paul talking? Is this a reference to a secret coming of Christ, as some claim about the popular text in Paul's letter to the Thessalonians? I would say, no, but you can judge for yourselves. Here is what I am thinking: If we read this, like we would any other text and not import ideas, we would take the ideas as Paul has already laid them out. He prefaced this mystery statement with the thought that the flesh cannot inherit what is ethereal. He took the time to write this idea in two different ways, to be sure we knew what he meant and that it was an important base for what he was going to say next. Thus, it seems quite right to assume that this "change," Paul is talking about, is a transformation from the mortal to the immortal – from flesh to spirit. In context, is there any other way to interpret this? In this passage alone, we are not seeing any talk of flying through the air or a secret coming of Jesus. The only talk here, so far, is about our mortality and the coming immortality. As we move on, we are told that this will happen at the "last trumpet." Now, as some scholars have done, we can begin to pull in other scriptures to try to explain this trumpet and the changes being made, but this may be an error in eschatology. Just because another text in the Bible mentions a trumpet, does not mean that trumpet is the same one. A trumpet is a musical instrument and does not need to carry the same overarching metaphoric meaning in every place it is mentioned. Trumpets were used in the Old Testament and they were not always the symbol of some deeper meaning. If we take the approach of always the same thing, then when we see the word "mountain" in the Bible we will need to always assign it the same meaning. After all, the word "mountain" is used symbolically in several places in God's Word, yet in many cases, the meaning is just that there was a physical mountain. So, let's be very careful, here.

What could this last trumpet be? Is it the last of the trumpets mentioned in Revelation? There is no reason to believe this trumpet is the same, and Revelation probably had not yet been written when Paul wrote this. There is one, possibly better, explanation for this mystery. As I said earlier, trumpets were a familiar sound at funerals. At the time of the disciples, trumpets had been used during funerals for a very long time. So, the last trumpet the dead would "hear" would be the one that they would never hear again. In a real sense, if the attendees of the funerals thought that the spirit of the dead person had not yet departed, then the dead person would "hear" that last trumpet sound. Even if the spirit had parted already (likely), those who were burying the dead would hear the trumpet (the last trumpet sound for that dead person), and the timing of it would be associated with the person departing this world for the next. In a Christian context, the person dies, their spirit departs to be with Jesus, and a trumpet announces their departure. This idea is similar to what pagans thought in Paul's day, and some non-Christians still believe it today. The idea is that when the body dies, the spirit departs and there is loud music or shouting to alert the after-world that they are coming. Thus, we see the significance of this whole scenario for Jews and gentiles – Christian or not.

What is interesting, here, is that after Paul talks about this instant change, he goes back and re-emphasizes his original point. He says,

> **"For the perishable must clothe itself with the imperishable, and the mortal with immortality. When the perishable has been clothed with the imperishable, and the mortal with immortality, then the saying that is written will come true: "Death has been swallowed up in victory."**

So, I think that without importing other ideas or texts into this passage, we can see that Paul has a pretty straightforward message. The flesh cannot obtain what is spiritual. We will become immortal, not by our means, but by the power of God. When this flesh dies, we will all be changed (not all at the same moment in history), and we will all become immortal, as God transforms us.

If we take this simple reading and this simple idea, then plug it into the text we studied in Thessalonians, that text is more easily understood. The Thessalonian text talks about similar ideas, though they are even more mysterious. Rather than going out on an eschatological limb and importing symbols and ideas from Revelation or elsewhere, we can keep within the same framework of Paul's teachings. His mannerisms were the same throughout his letters and what he taught was consistent. If we let Paul explain Paul, rather than importing other writers' symbolic prophecies, we might have a better idea of what these mysterious passages mean. At least this is the way I see it. You can be the judge.

Other Prophecies of the Apostles

There are at least 14 other Bible passages where the Apostles write prophetic messages. We can't go into depth on each one, but we can look at the major texts and see if there are any common themes. We may even gain some clarity by viewing what the early church was taught, overall.

First, let's look at the other prophetic texts that Paul wrote. Paul had more text about the future than other Apostles.

Romans 11:1-6

> **I ask then: Did God reject his people? By no means! I am an Israelite myself, a descendant of Abraham, from the tribe of Benjamin. 2 God did not reject his people, whom he foreknew. Don't you know what Scripture says in the passage about Elijah—how he appealed to God against Israel: 3 "Lord, they have killed your prophets and torn down**

**your altars; I am the only one left, and they
are trying to kill me"? 4 And what was God's
answer to him? "I have reserved for myself
seven thousand who have not bowed the knee
to Baal." 5 So too, at the present time there is
a remnant chosen by grace. 6 And if by
grace, then it cannot be based on works; if it
were, grace would no longer be grace.**

This passage in Romans deals with the question the disciples asked: When will the kingdom be restored to Israel? So, let's see if there is any added information here. Paul asks, did God reject his people? Paul says, no. Paul himself is an Israelite (tribe of Benjamin – seed of Abraham), and he is saved, thus a child of God – right? So if Paul is in the kingdom of heaven, then obviously, the Jews were not summarily thrown out of the kingdom. Paul recites a passage from the Old Testament where God reserved a remnant of true followers of God, though the majority had abandoned God. Paul shows a parallel principle about his generation. In verse 5, Paul says, "… at the present time," there is a remnant (of the Israelites) who have been chosen by God's grace (not by any works they have done).

So, what is the best conclusion here about Israel? Paul certainly did not get into the kingdom of heaven by his works. He was perfect as far as the Law. He was a Pharisee and a son of a Pharisee. However, all the sacrifices, tithes, and Law-keeping were of little good to save Paul. The one thing he had not done, was to accept and embrace Jesus as the Messiah. Thus, we must apply this same principle that Paul taught the early churches to Israelites today. A remnant is still reserved.

Of all those who are Israel by blood, only those who accept Jesus Christ are allowed into the kingdom of heaven – thus these are the only ones who belong to Christ and whose souls will be with God for eternity. Now, let's look at the next text that Paul wrote.

II Thessalonians 1:6-10

> **God is just: He will pay back trouble to those who trouble you 7 and give relief to you who are troubled, and to us as well. This will happen when the Lord Jesus is revealed from heaven in blazing fire with his powerful angels. 8 He will punish those who do not know God and do not obey the gospel of our Lord Jesus. 9 They will be punished with everlasting destruction and shut out from the presence of the Lord and from the glory of his might 10 on the day he comes to be glorified in his holy people and to be marveled at among all those who have believed. This includes you, because you believed our testimony to you.**

Do you see any familiar references here? You may not, if you have not read my book, REVELATION WITHOUT INFLAMMATION, however, this passage tends to mirror a lot of the text in Revelation. In both places, there are references to the destruction of God's enemies and those who hurt the believers. The question at this point is, when? Paul answers this also. He says,

> **"This will happen when the Lord Jesus is**
> **revealed from heaven in blazing fire with his**
> **powerful angels. 8 He will punish those who**
> **do not know God and do not obey the gospel**
> **of our Lord Jesus."**

Does this seem to line up with the prophetic words of Jesus?
From the way I read this, it does. Jesus foretells coming
trouble and destruction. Jesus talks about himself coming in
clouds to judge Israel for their sin and their rejection of God's
Son. Paul echoes this same message. Thus, we have
confirmation of the event and what this event looks like. Paul
then adds that they will be punished with the destruction that is
everlasting. Does this mean they will be tortured for eternity,
or does it mean that the nature of the destruction is permanent?
If it is permanent destruction, then the Israelites (as a people),
Jerusalem, and Judea would never be the same again. There
would be no "fixing" it – no true going back to what they once
were. However, if this is more of a permanent punishment – as
in everlasting torture in Hell, then it takes on another meaning.
So you will need to research this and apply RID rules, to figure
out what is meant by this text. Let's go now to the next
Pauline text, which is also in Thessalonians.

I Thessalonians 5:1-5

> **Now, brothers and sisters, about times and**
> **dates we do not need to write to you, 2 for**
> **you know very well that the day of the Lord**
> **will come like a thief in the night. 3 While**
> **people are saying, "Peace and safety,"**
> **destruction will come on them suddenly, as**

labor pains on a pregnant woman, and they will not escape. 4 But you, brothers and sisters, are not in darkness so that this day should surprise you like a thief. 5 You are all children of the light and children of the day. We do not belong to the night or to the darkness.

Let's make sure we do a Fresh Read here and then discuss this passage. What is your opinion? Again, I see the echo of Jesus' words. Jesus could not tell his disciples the dates and times of when he would return or any of the signs leading up to it. Why? Because he didn't know, but also because the meaning of the term "the end," was task or event oriented - not time oriented. In this passage, Paul says the "day of the Lord" will come like a thief in the night. Thus, the coming destruction will happen suddenly. One of Paul's purposes here is to give the church a warning so they would not be surprised when Jesus returned in judgment. Paul's comfort to the church came as a reminder that they were children of the light, and thus they would not be destroyed along with the children of darkness (disobedient unbelievers).

When we lay out this passage and use our R.I.D rules, one red flag pops up. The issue is the term "day of the Lord." This is a term we have not dealt with much. Is this synonymous with what Jesus calls his "return," or is this another time?

I did some brief research and so must you. Here is what I see: It seems this phrase "day of the Lord," is used over 30 times in the Bible, but mostly in the Old Testament. However, each time it is used, it is associated with God's judgment. When the term is used, it often includes surrounding text that talks about the wrath of God. Thus, I think we can rightfully estimate that in the New Testament, this phrase is also connected with the wrath and judgment of God. And, guess what? It is. When Jesus or the Apostles use this phrase it is about judgment. Can we make the right connection between Jesus' return and the "day of the Lord?" I believe we can. When it comes to a large judgment event, I see no other event Jesus or the Apostles talked about that could qualify as well as Jesus' return. Now, you read and study to see what you come up with, but I am pretty convinced - at least at this point.

Words of John

I John 2:18-19

> **Dear children, this is the last hour; and as**
> **you have heard that the antichrist is coming,**
> **even now many antichrists have come. This**
> **is how we know it is the last hour. 19 They**
> **went out from us, but they did not really**
> **belong to us. For if they had belonged to us,**
> **they would have remained with us; but their**
> **going showed that none of them belonged to**
> **us.**

What do you see in this short passage? To me, this is interesting, because John is proclaiming that it was the last hour. I have to say, wow. I have heard so many sermons and lectures that claim our generation was in the last hour. I must say, in light of this text, I have some serious doubts that John would have agreed. For a generation that lives 1900 years after him, how can we teach that John was speaking to us? He was writing to his fellow Christians of his day. Well, you read this again and see what you think. Without manipulating the text, it seems to me that John is addressing his generation and telling them that it was their last hour. I think we can rightfully say that this last hour was before the return of Christ, but this certainly points to the arrival of antichrists, which are signs of things that must happen before Christ's return.

I think the big point about the antichrist (or antichrists) is that Jesus seemed to emphasize there would be many imposters and false prophets emerging. It seems to me that John is pointing out the fulfillment of Jesus' prophetic words. On this basis, John proclaims twice in this passage that this is how they knew it was the last hour. Thus, this is not a passing comment - it is a declaration of proof for Jesus' soon return! And this declaration, again, does not seem to be for future generations – it is declared for John's generation. At least this is what I get when I just read it straight and fresh. See what you think.

Another thing I see here is that at least some of these antichrists had been members of the church. They "went out from us," John says. This could mean that they used their association with the church to gain credibility for their teachings. They may have gained a following within the church, and then proclaimed they were Jesus, and left the church, taking many followers with them. Sadly I have seen this happen many times in our local churches. Ministers within the church (who were not claiming to be Jesus), would get members to trust them, then use that influence to either try to take the church away from the current pastor or take their followers and start a new church elsewhere. In most cases, it was completely inappropriate and highly unethical in the clergy community.

Well, that is pretty much all there is in this passage. For being a short statement, it can be a very powerful tool for eschatological viewpoints. In light of this, we need to make sure we don't pull out short texts and use them to forward a huge montage of end-times doctrine. These types of passages need to stay in context and be considered along with larger teaching passages, as support. To take this passage and use it for doomsday preaching to today's church seems out of place. Even when our view is Futurist and Dispensational, we need to be very careful that we don't take time-sensitive textual content and import it to a time 2000 years later. It is just bad Bible interpretation and bad eschatology. Let's keep the original transcripts pure in our studies.

Words of Peter

2 Peter 3:3-10

> **Above all, you must understand that in the last days scoffers will come, scoffing and following their own evil desires. 4 They will say, "Where is this 'coming' he promised? Ever since our ancestors died, everything goes on as it has since the beginning of creation." 5 But they deliberately forget that long ago by God's word the heavens came into being and the earth was formed out of water and by water. 6 By these waters also the world of that time was deluged and**

**destroyed. 7 By the same word the present
heavens and earth are reserved for fire, being
kept for the day of judgment and destruction
of the ungodly. 8 But do not forget this one
thing, dear friends: With the Lord a day is
like a thousand years, and a thousand years
are like a day. 9 The Lord is not slow in
keeping his promise, as some understand
slowness. Instead he is patient with you, not
wanting anyone to perish, but everyone to
come to repentance. 10 But the day of the
Lord will come like a thief. The heavens will
disappear with a roar; the elements will be
destroyed by fire, and the earth and
everything done in it will be laid bare.**

This is an important text and deserves careful consideration.
Read it, freshly, and see what you see. It seems to me that
there were Christians in Peter's day who were not believing in
Jesus' return. The reasoning they were using was that nothing
had changed (that they could see, anyway) in their daily
routines or the nation. Because they refused to believe Jesus
was returning, they discarded their concern for living a good
and holy life and started living sensually. Of course, this was
against all Christian teaching anyway, but as we can see in our
current world when the "cat is not watching, the mice will
play." Perhaps this is why in our culture, preachers use
doomsday doctrines to try to keep people living Godly. Either
way, whether in Peter's day or ours, fear of Christ's return does
not produce a holy living. True commitment comes from a
Christian's heart and is born from a loving and close

relationship with Jesus. Nothing else stands the test of time or persecution.

The scoffers in Peter's day, asked, "Where is this coming he promised?" Peter points out how God destroyed the world with a flood, simply by his word. I think the point here is that the people of Noah's day also scoffed at Noah and his big boat. Nothing had changed and there were no obvious indicators that a huge flood was headed their way. Then, suddenly and without warning, it began to rain, the waters rose, and there was a deadly flood. Peter points out that similarly there was coming destruction – not by water, but by fire. In the same way, as the flood was used for judgment, the coming fire would be a tool of judgment. So, why did Peter mention this fire judgment? Is this a prediction of the end of the world? The flood was not the end of the world. God saved some, and the world went on. With the fire that was to come, if we use Peter's analogy, the ungodly are going to be destroyed, but the Godly would be kept safe. I am not sure how you take this all, but in light of Jesus' teaching (the one who taught Peter), this does not sound like a final judgment in heaven, and not a picture of Hell, either. This is beginning to sound a lot like what Jesus said was coming at the time of his return. See what you think.

Peter also brings in the aspect of the Lord's timing and perspective (a day is like a thousand years, etc.). It seems to me that God is timeless, that is, he seems to live outside of time and is not bound by it. If this is as it seems, God could move to any time frame at will and in essence, exist in all time at the same time as if it was today, to him. Perhaps this is why he introduced himself to Moses as the "I am." He is – he exists the same for all people at all eras of time. He knows the future because he is already there. Perhaps an eternal God must have this ability. If he always was and will always be, then time has no meaning for him or his existence. However, as interesting as this theory is, and though it has a basis in scripture, the bottom line is, we don't know all that much about God's makeup or what he can do. We only have a glimpse of him through what he has told us about himself – and this should be enough. So, our little theories here must remain that. We don't teach or preach any of these as facts. The point Peter was trying to make, though, is that God is not slow to keep his promise. He is patient. And let me remind readers again, that the Greek for "the end" is not time-based. It is task/event-based. God was going to complete everything he planned, regardless of how long it took.

Peter then echoes his Savior and says that Jesus' return and his judgment on the ungodly would be like a thief. It would not come with a heralding announcement. Then Peter reminds his readers that when Jesus returned, the heavens would disappear with a roar; the elements would be destroyed by fire, and the earth and everything done in it would be laid bare. This statement seems to be metaphoric. If the heavens actually disappeared as a result of this great destruction, the world would be uninhabitable. The same is true concerning the elements being destroyed by fire. No one could survive temperatures that melt all the metals in the soil. Yes, I know. I have been in the lectures and seen the movies. We could start saying, oh, this must be a nuclear bomb, but are we really going to go there? Reading this text straight and keeping it within the context of what Peter's master taught him, we must see that this judgment and Jesus' return had to happen within the disciples' generation, otherwise Jesus was a liar. And he is not. Jesus also said the believers would be spared, if they fled to the mountains for safety. They obeyed Jesus' instructions and were saved from the destruction of their region. To the disciples, what was destroyed was their whole world. Remember, the "world" was a lot smaller then than it is today.

I think this wraps up what Peter prophesied. For the less obvious words in this passage, make sure you follow the R.I.D rules. Look at the Greek and look up other passages that use similar phrasing. You will likely get more from this text by clarifying some of the symbolic phrases.

Chapter 14

Summary

In this last chapter, I want to pull together all the things we have talked about. If you think you have a good handle on it, then you may not find a lot of value in this review. If so, you can just skip over this and say "so long, and thanks." For readers who want to go over some ideas one more time, please read on.

One Last Story

During one of my writing sessions, my wife was watching a program that had a rather cheesy Elvis impersonator. I wasn't focused on what he was doing, but I did hear him make jokes about being "all shook up." So, I couldn't help but wonder what would happen if I told you about this incident and then added my own cheesy illustration. What I considered was something like this:

Just as the Elvis impersonator was "all shook up," some readers may have been all shook up when they discovered that some of Jesus' prophecies are not what they previously thought. Of course, I had some second thoughts about this and had to consider that taking something as important as Jesus' words, and launching them from lackluster performance by an Elvis look-alike, just seemed like a bad idea. So I decided not to use the impersonator's actions as an illustration. However, there is one interesting footnote in all this: When I first wrote the word, "illustration," I misspelled it and wrote "illustraction." Ironically, this whole Elvis discussion turned out to be exactly that - just a distracting illustration with little or no redeeming value. Yes, it is okay to laugh, now. ☺

Review – The Beginning

I have often taken the opportunity to point out the background of Dispensationalism and the Scofield Study Bible, so I will jump on this little soapbox again. Please remember when looking at commentaries on end-times, that many scholars are deeply influenced by Darby's teaching, and that Scofield was also influenced. Remember that Darby came on the scene in the late 1700s and early 1800s. He only started teaching his theories after he fell off of a horse (and bumped his head). Whether these events are connected, we don't know. It could just be a coincidence. The thing that is most important about Darby's doctrines is that no church before the early 1800s believed or taught them. When he introduced them they were considered heresy. Darby was thrown out of any groups he tried to influence. However, when a bright scholar decided to pen a study Bible with Darby's views, the popularity of

Darby's teachings gained solid ground. Years later, it became the most end-time teaching. It was not taught as just another view, it was taught as fact. In more recent times, Dispensationalism has escaped scrutiny, because there is a disclaimer about it being a doctrine. Literature on Dispensationalism says that it is a method of studying the Bible, not a doctrine. When I hear that and see how the study method is used, I see a very forced doctrine that is well protected among the clergy. If you dare to touch any part of it, you are declared a heretic and not a true believer in Christ. My question here, has to be this: How did the church go from treating Dispensationalism as heresy to embracing it as the "holy grail?" My position is this: Read the Bible straight without manipulating the text. Reading it literally, while imposing meanings from other verses that just do not apply, is not reading it literally. It is polluting the original manuscript. Also, taking things that are being presented in a dream or vision, and assigning a literal meaning to them just because God didn't reveal the meaning of the symbols, is just bad eschatology – and bad Bible study. So, be careful out there. Read the Bible similarly to how you would read any other book. Read what is on the page - consider when it was written - and to who it was written. There are logged history, poems, foretelling, and a lot of letters that were written to people, in the Bible. Consider the context and keep things in perspective. This is just a good, everyday reading technique for any book - religious or secular.

Parables

The first things we explored were some parables. Why? Because there is a lot of future-telling within the lessons of the parables. Do you remember anything from what you saw in that section?

What about Matthew 13:24-30? This is the story about a man who sowed good seeds, then an enemy came and sowed bad seeds in his field. It is a parallel lesson to show what the kingdom of God is like. The good plants and the weeds are allowed to live together in the field, then when they are harvested, they are separated, and the weeds are destroyed. The good seed seems to be the believers, and the bad seed seems to be the ungodly unbelievers. This is fairly significant in end-times teaching because this shows that there is both a saving of the righteous and destruction of the wicked.

One thing we stumbled on was the phrase "kingdom of heaven." Since this is not defined in this passage, we had to go searching to see if we could find what it means. This is what I found, summarized:

> **There are over 30 verses in the Bible that have the phrase "kingdom of heaven." However, it seems that only Matthew used this term. The term kingdom of God, or "of the Lord" is used in a few other places in the Bible, but in many places where God's kingdom is mentioned, it is just referred to as the Kingdom. As a side note: In Greek, it seems a kingdom that is from or in the "heavens" is a celestial idea. So, perhaps the phrase, kingdom of heaven, is more generic,**

> **where "kingdom of God" is (at least to the
> Jews) more specifically the heavenly kingdom
> that belongs to, or is ruled by Jehovah God.**

Possibly the biggest clue to what this phrase means comes from Matthew chapters 3, 4, 5, and 9. Here is where we learn that John the Baptist came preaching "Repent for the kingdom of heaven is near." After John was imprisoned, Jesus began to preach the same message, and when Jesus sent out his disciples, he told them to preach "The kingdom of heaven is near." So part of the gospel message seemed to include this idea that people needed to straighten out their lives and live in a Godly manner.

We also discussed a couple of other parables, but we don't need to go through the details of all of them. Some highlights of them include the fact that Jesus was clearly saying this "kingdom of heaven" or "of God," was on earth right then and there. He said it was among them and Jesus was the key representative of that kingdom. As far as the remaining parables, most of them deal with similar issues. There are more lessons on how the believers and unbelievers are sorted out and how the unbelievers are destroyed.

Matthew's Account of Jesus' Words

We went through most of what Matthew wrote about Jesus' prophetic words. They are found mostly in Matthew, chapter 24. The passage seems to begin with the disciples admiring the temple's structural beauty. Jesus follows by saying that all the beautiful stones and their adornment would be torn down. Of course, the disciples were disturbed by this news, and they asked Jesus when it was going to happen, and if there were any signs they could watch for, to indicate when this destruction was about to happen. Jesus answered them with a surprising amount of information. He even told them that when they saw one of the signs (desecration of the temple), they needed to leave the area immediately and flee to the safety of the mountains. One of the more important messages Jesus gave the disciples was that all the things he told them would occur within their generation. None of what Jesus said to his disciples in chapter 24, seemed to stretch beyond their lifetimes.

Mark's Account of Jesus' Words

When we compared Mark, chapter 13 to what Matthew wrote, we found a lot of the same verbiage and ideas. There were no doctrinal differences between them. Mark's account is a little shorter than Matthew's, so there are some things in Matthew that are not in Mark. No foul - no problem.

Luke's Account of Jesus' Words

In Contrast, Luke seems to give a fairly detailed version of what Jesus said. When Luke, chapter 21, is compared to Matthew 24 and Mark 13, however, there is little to worry about in differences. They all agree on doctrinal content, and again, I see no definite content of what Jesus said that indicates his prophecies extended beyond the life of the disciples.

The Apostles Words

When we got down to studying the letters of Paul, John, and Peter, we noticed that there were several prophetic passages. Paul had the most content, but this should not be surprising, since there are many more of Paul's letters in the Bible than any other Apostle.

We found that in the book of Thessalonians some text could be used to support Rapture and possibly some aspects of Dispensationalism. At the same time, another text in Thessalonians, that was similar, left a lot of questions about rising from the dead and eternity with Jesus.

Looking into Romans and Corinthians there seemed to be some associated ideas about resurrection, and eternal life. All in all, there seemed to be an agreement, doctrinally, among the three Apostles. They used slightly different words and different approaches, but the ideas were the same. Under scrutiny, it seemed to me that at least 90% of what was said was referencing events that were to happen in their lifetime. The remaining 10% or less, is just not very clear. These we are leaving as a mystery that God has likely not revealed to us.

I suppose this wraps up most of what we found. Was it exciting? Maybe, maybe not, but it was very important to look at these texts without imported ideas. I think we may have uncovered a few things and blown the smoke away from a lot of the confusion about end-times prophecies.

Some Other Warnings

After doing this "Fresh Read," you may want to know more. Perhaps you want to know how other scholars have interpreted

Jesus' words - and you may want to know what resources are available to help you study independently. To address this, I first want to caution you about reading Bible commentaries. You need to make sure you have a base of knowledge that is independent of others' thinking before you plunge into the depths of others' speculation. However, once you are pretty sure of what the text says, and what it doesn't say, then you can start to review other scholars' thinking and make sensible evaluations of their beliefs. Of course, there are a ton of books and commentaries on Jesus' words. Perhaps the best place to start is to look at the ones that have been written by very learned scholars. When a person has studied many different aspects of a book (such as historical events, culture, and language of the time) and taken a lot of time in doing it, you will likely find their writings and insights more valuable than the writings of shallow and whimsical authors.

Before I continue with study discussions, I'd like to interject one message. In this book, I've purposely avoided deep study. Like never before, I wanted you to look at what the Bible text is really saying. I wanted you to gain a ground-roots view of what Jesus said, and to shed yourself of anything else you have heard about his prophecies. This is part of "truth" learning; that is, not true learning, but truth-learning. As others have said, when we offer our pet doctrines on the "Altar of Truth," the true doctrines, survive the fire and the false ones, perish. What we want is the truth. As we dig into scripture, we need to separate faddish and traditional beliefs from what the Bible truly says. The important and key doctrines of the Bible are repeated and reinforced by specific directions, and by examples. This may be because God wants to make his salvation crystal clear to even simple-minded people. In this book, I also wanted to try very hard not to influence you to a single way of thinking. My purpose with this book is not to make you believe the way I do or teach others the things I've speculated about. I want you to know how to practice good and untainted eschatology (at an entry-level). I want you to be able to look at the Bible with different eyes and a different mindset; to use some basic rules; and to see what God was trying to communicate. As always, one of the more important aspects of a good study is keeping things in context. What did the author start to say way before the verse you are reading? What did he say, right after and way after the verse? For instance, if Jesus began talking about sacrificing our lives for The Kingdom - talks about relationships - and then talks more about the sacrificial life, then we can properly and rightfully deduce that Jesus' reference to relations was not as much a lesson about friends as it was about sacrifice (not saying Jesus taught this exact thing. It is a hypothetical example). Please read wider areas of text when you are studying and try to capture the author's overall point as well as the specific verse-to-verse point. When you do this, you will better understand the one who penned it.

Guessing Should Not Be Believing

Should we ever believe something that is based on a guess? Do we do that with end-time prophecies? Do we take someone's best guess and say, well that's good enough for me? If so, it is tragic and can lead to believing absolute heresy. God always says what he means, and if he wants us to truly know, he will make it plain as the fingers on your hand.

God never provided prophecy so we could march out on a wild goose chase. In most cases, prophecies were promises. God said I am going to do this – and you can count on it. God's future telling has frequently held both good and bad things; restoration and destruction. The people who were there at the time may have (at least partially) understood what God foretold, but when the prophecy was fulfilled, there was little doubt. If Jesus' prophecies are about our future (and there is some possible doubt there), then trying to figure out all of what will happen is not going to work well. What we need to do is study the prophecy and remember it. Then when the time comes, we will see it unfold and say, "Hey, that's what God meant!" The danger of trying to nail down prophecy is exemplified by what happened before Jesus' time. The leaders and students of the law thought the messiah would come in a specific way. They were so locked into a certain way of thinking that when he came they missed him. Whatever God has planned for our future, if we do the same and become so rigid in our thinking about Jesus' prophecies, we very well may miss his glorious work and the time, or times of his appearing.

Best Use of the Book

So, what is the best use of Jesus' prophetic words? Perhaps we should start with an overarching approach to the Spiritual view. Prophecy teaches us many things about God's love for us and how important it is to follow him. There are great rewards for obedience and terrible consequences when we diametrically oppose him. We can move from there to accept that God has many things planned for our future. They may or may not be described in typical prophecies, but we can know for sure that if God planned good things for his church in the first century, he also planned good things for those in his church, today. And, maybe it doesn't matter how we are transported to where God dwells. Whether we become human rockets and fly to meet him; or breathe our last breath while lying in a bed - does it really matter? The joy is being with Jesus, our groom, for all eternity. Yes, it is more exciting to think about going out in a kind of epic cosmic bang rather than enduring the sufferings of old age - but shouldn't our focus be on where we spend eternity rather than the method of arriving there?

What else can we see about Jesus' words? We can admit that God has worked with men and nations these last 2000 years. There have been marvelous miracles and widespread revivals that affected whole cities (occasionally countries). Even in our era, there's a revival in China, with tens of thousands coming to Christ, every month. There are documented stories of new converts from Islam to Christianity; because Jesus appeared to someone and called them to himself. God is still working to bring people into the Kingdom and he will not stop until all have come in that he desires.

Did, Jesus already come one time? Some say yes and some say no, but again, does it matter? Who is to say there are only two appearances of Christ? I see no place in scripture that disallows Jesus to come whenever and however he likes. He is God! Considering this, some people can follow false Christs – so we need to be very vigilant. As far as the real Christ revealing himself to people or visiting them, I am sure it has happened hundreds of times. The truth is that the Spirit of Christ is alive and well on planet earth and he is working, every day. If there is a physical end to this earth (and there very well may be someday), then God will be as much in control of that as he has been with every other major event on this planet. What we need to do is trust him. In the meantime, we can consider what Paul wrote to Timothy on this topic:

2 Timothy 3:16 "All Scripture is God-breathed and is useful for teaching, rebuking, correcting and training in righteousness ..."

So, what's the best use of Jesus' words? It is the same as any other scripture. It is from God; we pay attention and heed all the warnings; we read it and remember it; and if a prophecy unfolds, we respond to it according to the instructions given in the prophecy. When we teach it, we teach it for knowledge. This means that if it has happened already, we learn the lessons that perhaps the people at the time of the prophecy didn't. If it is for the future, we learn the lesson of paying attention to what God has said and making sure we are complying with what God has asked us to do. So as you can see, whether a prophecy was for people in the past, or us and our future, the result is the same. We apply what we hear to our lives and cling close to our savior who sacrificed all to redeem us.